# A HANDY, ONE-VOLUME GUIDE . . .

. . . to the sport and recreation of motorcycling: this book, written by top experts in the field, is just that!

Beginning with a description of the latest available models—including mini-bikes—and ending with action portraits of today's exciting champions, it brings a wealth of practical information to all cycle fanciers—from the teen-ager planning the purchase of his first bike to the veteran competitor.

THE MOTORCYCLE AND TRAIL BIKE HANDBOOK is indispensable—complete, authoritative, and up-to-the-minute!

# THE

# MOTORCYCLE

## AND

# TRAIL BIKE

# HANDBOOK

●

**BOB BEHME**
and
**MALCOLM JADERQUIST**

PYRAMID BOOKS • NEW YORK

**THE MOTORCYCLE AND TRAIL BIKE HANDBOOK**

A PYRAMID BOOK

Pyramid edition published April, 1971

PYRAMID BOOKS are published by Pyramid Publications
A Division of the Walter Reade Organization, Inc.
444 Madison Avenue, New York, New York 10022, U.S.A.

# TABLE OF CONTENTS

# *FOREWORD*

BY VIRTUE of their special design, motorcycles offer several distinct advantages over automobiles. Better visibility. You can see in all directions without obstruction. Better maneuverability. You can turn and stop quickly to avoid obstacles you might not miss with a car. Faster reaction times. The rear brake pedal is near one foot and the front brake is at your fingertips. Superior braking. Most cycles can stop faster than the best car.

In contrast, however, there are drawbacks. Cycles are more vulnerable. Riders do not have the protection of an automobile. Road conditions are more demanding. It is harder to retain control on poor roads. And cycling requires a special attitude. The person who assumes "I can drive a car so I can ride a bike" may be headed for trouble.

It is our hope to reduce the difficulties and accentuate the positive. If we can keep one rider out of trouble or help another find pleasure he might not have discovered, this book will have done all we hoped it would do.

Portions of this book were checked for accuracy by several people expert in their field. The authors are grateful for the help but assume full responsibility for all errors. We are grateful to the American Motorcycle Association for permission to adapt portions of their most informative booklet, "Forming a Club," in our chapter on clubs and to Yamaha International for permission to use portions of their fine booklet, "Common Sense Tips for Safe Sports-cycling," in our chapter on riding.

BOB BEHME
MALCOLM JADERQUIST

*Magalia, California*

Chapter 1

## CHOOSING YOUR MOTORCYCLE

IF YOU ARE READY to buy your first motorcycle, chances are you have a problem. How do you find the right machine?

After buying a number of bikes I'm convinced that you'll have to go through a number of definite steps. You must first define the kind of riding you want to do. Then you must choose the kinds of bike that fits that riding, street, trail, etc. You must discover the various makes and models that fit that criteria and then the actual prices, as opposed to the advertized costs. Finally, you must make your choice, based first on the data you've gathered and then on the basis of the local dealer with the best after-sales service.

*Street Machine*     In the past the most popular model, the street machine is equipped with a high rpm engine whose power is delivered only within a narrow rpm band. Acceleration is guaranteed through the use of a close-ratio transmission. Most manufacturers use four-speed gear boxes but some engines require five- and six-speed cases. The steering geometry is designed for stability and easy steering at highway speeds. The suspension is "soft" with very little travel. The fuel tank is large to give you mileage between fuel stops and the fenders are low to keep you dry on rainy days. The bike is fully street legal with all required equipment from dual foot pegs to headlights.

Until a few years ago few street bike buyers were not aware of the 350cc class, but that is changing. Now many feel the 250cc machines are underpowered and the 500's too ponderous and bulky. The in-between bikes, the 350's, are coming up fast.

*Street/Scrambler*     Less of a definite category than in past seasons, the street/scrambler has enough rough terrain equipment to handle dirt roads and trails. It differs from a straight street bike in several ways. The exhaust pipe is usually swept up. The engine has improved ground clearance, and the gas tank is smaller. In some versions the street/scrambler is lighter than a street machine, the engine slightly detuned to increase its power range.

The bike is fully street legal, that is, equipped with lights and muffler plus extra foot pegs and space for a passenger. Many include electric starters. The stock tire is a street tire and for semitrail use it's advisable to switch to a trails-universal, a modified knobby that works well on light trails.

*Woods/Trail*     Take a serious look at the woods/trail machine when you want something better suited to the really rugged back country. Sportsmen find the bike invaluable and cattlemen use it to patrol fences. The U.S. Forest Service even has a few. The cycle can be used for short city jaunts but it is not designed to work as a touring or commuting machine.

A major difference between the woods/trail and street bike is the woods/trail's relatively stark appearance. Nonessentials have been stripped away. The bike is designed to ride higher and some models offer nine or ten inches of clearance. The front fender is mounted higher above the wheel to avoid clogging and some manufacturers use fiberglass and plastic fenders and fuel tanks to save more weight.

The front forks and rear suspension are designed to absorb the exaggerated trail shocks and because of it have a look that differs from street/scrambler machinery. On a woods/trail the suspension has more travel than in a street cycle to help smooth out the rough trails.

Handlebars are wide for easy steering and the fuel tank is slender so a rider can stand on the pegs easily.

*Trail Bike*     Characterized by a low-revving engine with good power at the lower end. The ideal machine delivers muscle from idle to top rpm but any bike with a wide band of power is acceptable. Maximum horsepower is less important than on a street machine, but pulling power is basic.

A wide-ratio gear box is essential. Low gear must be low and the other gears should be widespaced—that is, with definite steps so that you can increase or decrease speed considerably before changing gears. The frame should be lightweight. The steering should be faster than on a street machine—that is, more responsive so the machine will change directions quickly as you shift your weight.

The front forks and rear shocks should have considerable travel, as with the woods/trail bike, and the front forks should be of a contemporary design. Ceriani types are generally considered best. The longer suspension travel will allow you to speed over rough ground while the bike itself absorbs shocks that might otherwise throw you off the machine.

*Choosing Engines*     Street cycles are equipped with engines from less than 50cc displacement to nearly 1200. To about 50cc's you can choose between two- and four-stroke and single- and twin-cylinder designs. The advantages of two- and four-stroke types have been enumerated many times and there is no reason to repeat them. Both are good. Most twins run smoother, with less vibration, but a twin has more parts and may cost more when you buy it and when you need to repair it. The advantages and drawbacks even out. Essentially, both types are good.

Do not choose a small cycle if you want a street machine. You may think a 50–125cc machine will be easier to ride, but it won't be. A 250cc cycle is only slightly harder to handle and the difference will only be noticeable for the first quarter of an hour. If you are of average weight a 50cc bike will pull you along at 35-40mph and a 125 will at about 55-60mph. A good 250cc should top 85-90mph and will cruise easily at 65 all day.

Who makes the best cycles? There is no single answer. In the past the Japanese were noted for the excellence of their small two-cycles and the best 250cc machine in the world. The Spanish and Italians were noted for sticking-in-the-corner racing bikes and the 650cc field belonged to the British. The really big touring bikes were German and American. Now its anybody's game. The Japanese are offering top machines in all sizes and the Americans and British are coming up fast.

*Buying a Used Bike* Motorcycles, like automobiles, have seasonal prices and the cost of a used bike depends in part on the time of year in which you buy. During the summer you are competing with many buyers and the best machines command top dollar. But if you buy late in the season, during the fall and winter, prices are lower and the selection may be even better.

You can buy from either a private party or a dealer. Both have advantages. Generally you will get your best cash deal from a private party. The fellow has neither overhead nor salesman's commissions to pay. The price is usually lower and the bike sells faster. But there are no guarantees and no after-sales service. If the cycle has problems, the problems are yours.

If you know enough about motorcycle mechanics to thoroughly check equipment, or if you know someone who does, purchasing from a private party may offer the best chance for a bargain. But if you are new to motorcycling, stick with a dealer. A used machine then is as reputable as the dealer. The better dealers have used machines checked and repaired by their service department before sale.

If you know the complete mechanical history of a used machine you're in a position to know what reconditioning is required. But if you have any doubts, or if the machine is unknown as it would be on a dealer's lot, check these major points before you buy:

**1.** *First impression* Does the bike look clean and cared for? A machine that is rough and dirty may have been ridden hard and carelessly. Check the speedometer. High mileage may indicate early repairs. If the mileage is low and there is fresh paint or new parts be doubly wary. The speedometer may be incorrect, the cycle has been ridden hard or has been in an accident.

**2.** *Test the engine* The engine should start easily and should sound in good condition. If there are unusual noises choose another bike or have this one checked by a competent, nonpartisan mechanic.

**3.** *Check the frame* Look for dents, cracks and bends. Be sure the welds are solid and the paint in reasonable condition. Check other items such as foot pegs, chain and sprocket for rust and excessive wear. If parts need replacement the bike may still be a good buy, but remember the costs increase the price of the cycle. Is the bike worth it?

**4.** *Check the tires*     Tires are an indicator of age, wear and care. Do they agree with the speedometer? If not, perhaps the bike has been ridden harder or longer than the mileage indicates. Old rubber, cracked or bald tires should be replaced. Tubes may be patched, but check them before you buy. Scratched or pinched tubes should be replaced.

**5.** *Check cables*     Be sure they are in good condition, neither worn nor pinched. If strands are bent or broken, cables may need replacement. Double check.

*Riding a Safe Bike*     If you want to be a safe rider you must ride safe equipment. A regular maintenance plan will guarantee that any bike, new or used, will be safe and reliable. Follow this eleven-point checklist.

**1.** *Check the lights*     The law requires at least one white headlight and one red taillight, each visible at a distance of 500 feet. Test all lights before you ride. Be sure that high and low beams work properly. If anything is wrong replace the light bulbs.

**2.** *Check the horn*     A horn increases a bike's safety. Be sure yours works.

**3.** *Check all bolts*     Check all bolts when you buy your cycle and regularly thereafter. Nuts and bolts may eventually work loose and some are difficult to replace because of an unusual combination of threads, length, material or finish.

**4.** *Check tire inflation*     Be sure the tires are properly inflated. Buy a tire gauge and use it. A correctly inflated tire increases the handling qualities of any machine.

Check rims and spokes monthly. Spokes should be tight. Tap each with a screwdriver to discover any loose ones. A loose spoke makes a dull sound; a tight one sings. Spokes that are too tight will eventually snap from the tensile load and may damage the inner tube. A rim should not be out of round more than 1/16th inch nor wobble from side to side more than the same distance. If a wheel is out have the dealer true it and balance it.

**5.** *Check rear visibility*    A cycle should have one good rearview mirror. It is good practice to use it often while you are riding and to verify what you see by turning your head when safety permits.

**6.** *Check the brakes*    Put the bike on its center stand, then balance it so that first one wheel and then the other is off the ground. Spin both wheels. Each should move easily and freely without friction or drag. Apply the brakes lightly as the wheel spins. It should stop promptly without wobble or side play.

If you can stop your bike within the distance required for an automobile, your brakes are working properly. But if they skip, fade or fail under hard braking, something is wrong. Many problems are caused by improperly adjusted cables. Set yours according to the instructions in your operator's manual. If the brakes do not work properly after adjustment have your dealer check them immediately.

**7.** *Check the chain*    Be sure the chain is properly adjusted and lubricated. On most cycles the rear chain should have about ½ inch of give or "play" when the cycle is off the stand.

**8.** *Check the battery*    Inspect the water level frequently and if fluid is needed, use distilled water only.

**9.** *Check clutch and transmission*     Check the clutch to prevent your cycle from "creeping" at stop lights. Adjustments are generally made at the lever and at the point at which the cable enters the clutch housing. Also be sure the engine and transmission have an adequate supply of oil.

**10.** *Check the fuel tank*     Be sure all connections are tight and leakproof. When you fill the tank avoid filling it to the rim. Gas spills can be dangerous on a hot engine.

**11.** *Check the lock*     Prevent theft. Motorcycles are easily stolen. Be sure to lock your bike every time you park. Carry fire, theft, comprehensive and liability insurance.

Chapter 2

## MOTORCYCLE ROUNDUP:

## A Summary of all 1971 Motorcycles

NINETEEN-SEVENTY was a vintage year both for the
manufacturers who built bikes in record numbers and
for the riders who bought them equally fast. Seventy-
one may be even better, for the cycles offered this season
are closer to the machines many riders say they really
want.

There are three major trends developing: the increased popularity of the super-bike, the demise of the
street/scrambler in favor of more practical street and
enduro machinery, and an end to redundant machinery
(for example, four or five machines in one displacement varied only in styling and inconsequential detail).

The super-bike bracket—only a few years ago restricted to Harley-Davidson, BMW, BSA, Triumph, and
a few others—has exploded to include almost half the
names in the field. Mid-1971 will see a 750cc machine
from Augusta with some fantastic statistics to back it
up—including a $3,900 price tag. BMW, never out of
the market, has a new 750. BSA's Rocket 3 now heads
the line, which still includes several 650's and a 500cc
bike. Benelli has an Italian 650 while Paul Dunstall, in
addition to his unique 750cc street-road racers, now
makes a 750 Gran Tourer and an out-of-the-crate
750cc road racer. Harley-Davidson, whose 900cc
Sportsters and 120cc Electra Glide are American insti-

tutions, has crossed the two to produce the 1200cc Super Glide.

The big bike ranks were further swollen by Honda's super 750cc four and the 500cc Mach III from Kawasaki. Moto Guzzi has their 750cc Ambassador, Munch discontinued their one and only machine, but Norton, another British big-bike standby, has five 750's from which to choose. The Rickman-Metisse series has a kit that will accept any of several standard British big displacement engines. It also includes a street machine that comes ready made with a 750cc Royal Enfield engine, although Royal Enfield is no longer available in the United States.

Triumph's Trident 750cc three, the Velocette 500's and Yamaha's new super 650 wrap up the American big bike field.

It is difficult to tell whether the availability of big bikes of this caliber created the demand for them or vice versa. But the point is academic since both the demand and the abundant supply of good machines are an integral part of the current bike scene.

It amazes me, when I think of such things, that an abortion with as many drawbacks as the old street/scrambler was able to generate enough interest to precipitate the present motorcycle boom. The category was a loose one but generally included a street frame with high pipes, a bash plate, and a good street engine slightly detuned (seldom detuned enough to spread the power band below 5000 rpm's, yet always enough to rob it of the snappy throttle response characteristic of a good street machine).

But the bike was popular and for a long time was the mainstay of the growing U.S. market. This year their replacements are either street bikes, enduros or both.

There was some consternation among new buyers

who wanted to know whether the discontinuation of street/scramblers meant that riders who rode on the street and in the rough must now buy two bikes. The answer is *no*. Any street bike will handle beautifully on dirt roads and trails and most enduro machines will ride admirably on the street. Most are street legal.

Many manufacturers have also extended their street and enduro lines. The street machines in such cases are the calmer products of the firm's racers and the enduro line has moved in two directions. One side offers competition scramblers with more power and better handling; the other offers trail machines. Neither of these machines are meant for street use but both are ideal for the enduro rider.

The third trend, the elimination of some models, may seem contradictory to the second. If one street/scrambler is dropped only to become two bikes—one for the street and another for the enduro—the total number of bikes must have increased. And it has. But there is an explanation. In the past years many builders were producing several machines with only slightly varying capabilities (street/trail, street/scrambler, trail/scrambler, *ad infinitum*). This year the poorer experiments are gone—the street/scramblers are dead, the repetitions are out. In their place are the super-bikes.

The 1971 machines are exciting. It is as one copywriter said: "This is probably the best year to buy a bike." For once the guy is right—and so is the market.

## AJS *(See chart #1)*

The name goes back a long way to an honorable, rugged and fast cycle, but the machine has been out of the picture for some time. It made its reappearance midway through the 1970 season and began winning races immediately. Ordinarily a new bike goes through some sorting out the first two years and is ready to be

considered a serious contender only in its third year.
But the AJS is different, because it is the offspring of
the Norton-Villers company, a group who dominated
dirt racing until the onslaught of two strokes.

Some engine development and frame modification has
resulted in the launching of two very hot models, alike
except for engine size.

The frame is a cross between a spine and cradle.
The backbone is a very thick, rigid piece of steel taper-
ing back to a spot under the seat. Smaller down tubes
cradle the engine and return to the opposite end of the
spine piece. It's a very effective arrangement.

The suspension is provided by Ceriani-type, oil-
dampened telescopic forks in front and Girling shocks
on a rear swing arm. The rims are chrome steel, and in
the interest of lightness and strength, the hubs are
conical.

The bikes have better than 9 inches of ground clearance, and the slightly heavier 370 model weighs only
230 pounds while putting out 33 horsepower.

As little brothers to the Norton Commando they will
become very popular in a short time.

## AMERICAN EAGLE (*See Chart #2*)

1970 was American Eagle's final production year.
The nine models shown in our chart are no longer
offered—except on the used market. But their high
horsepower to low weight ratio, careful design and good
construction should have made the bikes big sellers.
They weren't, and no one knows precisely why.

But the cycles are available as used machines and we
can recommend them. An American Eagle in good condition is still a bike to be reckoned with.

## AUGUSTA (*See Chart #3*)

Augusta is best known for road-racing machines,

and for good reason. With a three-cylindered cycle Agostini won several big European races. Last year M. V. Augusta won the World Championship in the 350 and 500cc classes with hot, specially built machines. Most of the winning qualities of Augusta racing bikes have filtered down to the production street machines. All have five-speed transmissions. Your choice of Augusta should depend only on the top speed you want.

The midyear will see a brand-new Augusta on the market. Few details are available now, but you can expect 76 horses at 7900 rpm's and a top speed of 140 miles per hour from 750cc's.

## BMW (*See Chart #4*)

There is but one reason BMW makes cycles: touring —the very best touring at that. The three models come to America with telescopic front forks, but they are available in Europe with Earles forks (and offered here on special order). The Earles are the firm's traditional forks and the ones used when sidecars are attached.

The 750, new last year, has already made a big name for itself. In addition to carrying on the BMW tradition, it has improved the firm's image by adding zero to 60 acceleration in just over six seconds.

In European racing, BMW side hacks own nearly every record available. The touring record for the stock bikes is even more impressive, including a New York-to-Los Angeles speed record and a run from Alaska to Tierra Del Fuego, South America's southernmost tip.

The most famous facet of BMW's reputation is reliability. It has been built into every machine and the new ones are no exceptions. Characteristic is the use of a drive shaft in place of a chain and the noiseless efficiency of the horizontally opposed cylinders. New is surprising throttle response and easier shifting. If old BMW's made owners happy the new models will make them ecstatic.

## BENELLI (See Chart #5)

The Italian manufacturer has taken it upon itself to build both a successful enduro machine and a good super-bike.

Their enduro is the 250cc Supersport. It offers a comfortable saddle over a great suspension system composed of Ceriani-type telescoping front forks and a three-way adjustable rear suspension. Thirty horses are conveyed through a five-speed transmission to the knobby-equipped rear wheel. The bike has a claimed top speed of 100mph and a total weight of 245 pounds. It accomplishes the first of Benelli's objectives admirably.

To accomplish the second objective, the firm brought out the Tornado. With a 650cc engine it qualifies as a *big* bike. The power plant delivers 50 horses and Benelli puts them through a five-speed transmission so effectively you can expect a top speed of 118mph. The bike weighs slightly more than 400 pounds—light enough to handle well yet heavy enough to qualify as a roadworthy tourer.

## BRIDGESTONE (See Chart #6)

Bridgestone still makes some machines reminiscent of the old street/scramblers, but their street machines are 100 percent street ready. Perhaps the problem is that other models are merely street bikes dressed with an upswept exhaust and a trail sprocket.

Whatever the problem, we are not excited by the dirt versions. Yet if you are looking for a good street bike, especially at a good price, take a long look at Bridgestone. Dollar for dollar it is a grand buy.

The GTR is an excellent example. Its engine is a sound two-stroke with a rotary valve. The twin cylinder design, typical of all winning 2-strokes, is capable of delivering 40 horses from 349cc's. With a relatively heavy curb weight of 337 pounds, the GTR has a quarter-mile record of 14.5 seconds and 89.4 miles per hour. Its top end is a bit over 100mph and with six speeds it gets there quickly. Several private riders with an eye for figures have put all these facts together and are happily racing Bridgestones.

## BSA *(See Chart #7)*

BSA came out with five surprises this year. All should be super-hot sellers. They were designed in part by factory racer John Banks—he should be given credit for doing a fine job.

The frames are roughly the same: a single down-tube cradle that splits into two parts as the cylinder barrel meets the crankcase. The models have conical hubs, telescopic forks and an exhaust pipe tucked neatly inside the frame. The 441, which replaced an old-fashioned 500cc single cylinder 4-stroke, has been replaced by a brand new 500cc single cylinder 4-stroke engine. The engine has undergone several beneficial changes, and is now a beautiful piece of machinery.

Yet differences are few. The SS bikes have 18-inch rims front and rear, while the dirt models have light alloy 20-inch rims in front. The motocross model has a smaller gas tank.

News from the factory recently centered around the 750cc, three-cylindered Trident. BSA was so confident of its abilities they simply uncrated a stock bike, added road racing tires and, without further preparation, set three new speed records.

The bike was hailed as the beginning of a new era in racing. In the past, 650cc twins were incapable of allow-ing heavy men to compete with lighter riders. The Trident has succeeded and although it may sound insignificant, the difference has opened the racing field.

Other talk centered around a special experimental rocket styled by the American designer Craig Vettor. The prototype is beautiful, and if the future holds more of the same, the future may belong to BSA.

## BULTACO (*See Chart #8*)

Señor Bulto, owner of Bultaco, broke away from Montesa during a feud over priorities. He wanted to design racing machines while Montesa wanted to concentrate on multi-use cycles. The result was that Señor Bulto began his own race-oriented company.

His first machines were road racers, fast yet nothing to set the world on fire. Even the basic engine was little more than a traditional two-cycle single. When additional racing made it evident that Bultaco's most efficient application was on dirt, the machine began making a name.

But once that pattern was set and once Bultaco had its super 250cc bike, all that remained was for the world to find out. Which it did when a field of hot 500cc four strokes saw nothing but the rear fender of the smaller, faster cycle. After the dust had settled the losers discovered they had been beaten by a machine half the size of their own. Converts were made with lightning speed.

Although they now share their position with manufacturers running large displacement two-stroke singles, Bultaco is still one of the best-known machines in racing. And for the nonracer, they build great enduros.

I like the Campera, detuned to produce 14 horses at 5500 rpm's. The figure indicates a broad power range, and that is exactly what the Campera has. I've ridden one over every type of terrain, lugging it, then winding the engine to what for most machines would be the breaking point, and have been rewarded with a great ride.

If I wanted to talk about their racing bikes, from 100cc's to 360cc's, I could go on forever—so long has been their string of successes. But of particular interest to riders who like dirt is the Montadero.

It was brought out last year, after the 360cc competition scrambler had been a success. Built like its predecessor, the Montadero enduro, it is detuned from 43 horses to about 32½, stretching the power band to accommodate the nonprofessional rider.

The rear swing arm has been shortened (with a compensating extension on the frame) for improved weight distribution. The only sacrifice required to accomplish this traction-improving move was a slight reduction in ground clearance; since the bike was more than nine inches, Bultaco remains among the very best.

The overall weight is 270 pounds, which makes the machine very maneuverable in the woods and stable on the road.

## CIMATTI *(See Chart #9)*

Cimatti offered five bikes last year, the wildest a 100cc flat-tracker. This year the old machines are gone and in their place are ten diverse models that will appeal to everyone.

If you like bikes, it's hard to feel an affinity for the Moped, so in this book we will consider the 1.27hp Chic as pure transportation.

The Sport is another matter. It is designed for the road and although small, is an exciting machine. Its engine puts out six horsepower and nestles within a double cradle frame painted silver-gray. The fenders, shocks, rims, carb, header and exhaust pipe, engine cover, front forks, clip-ons, headlight and gas cap are all chromed. The red gas tank with yellow racing stripes (both bright) sits in front of a two-step racing seat. And once you have included the road racing tires in that list, you have no more weight.

The bike looks fast and *is* fast when carrying light passengers. There isn't another machine quite like this one.

A few words should be mentioned about the Cross Competizione, especially the 175cc version, which is impressive. Its 19.5 horsepower boasts quite enough power to carry even the largest rider at a good clip. Although not big enough to challenge serious racing machines, it is a bike with the ingredients of a good competitor.

## DUCATI *(See Chart #10)*

Ducati has dropped the small bikes from its line and is concentrating on the three middle-range machines that enjoy much popularity. Of all their achievements the most noteworthy is the Desmodromic valve system. That's what makes their racing efforts notable. The design opens and closes the valves mechanically, permits a nearly limitless top end and eliminates valve float.

Ducati enduros are big singles that will lug down and wind tight with a great deal of power control. Their size makes them nearly ideal dual purpose machines.

The 450 is a prime rig for the rider who once had only the old BSA Victor. It's that kind of cycle.

## DUNSTALL *(See Chart #11)*

When the slowest machine has a top speed of 128 miles an hour, how do you describe the line? Of course the bikes are fast—the basic statistics illustrate that fact without help. But what few readers may know is that the bikes are reliable.

Most novices believe that fast, high output machinery

is unreliable. Not so. Paul Dunstall has built several different fast, powerful machines that last and last and last.

He starts with work bikes from Triumph and Norton and laboriously rebuilds them—his way. That means slowly, perfectly and without pressure. It takes from eight to ten weeks to get a Dunstall. The parts are not stock, but Dunstall-designed and -tested over the nine years he has been in business. Paul does such a thorough rebuilding job that the British Government has registered his firm's name as a manufacturer.

In addition to the five cycles listed, Dunstall builds one racer. It has a special "spine frame," a reworked 74 horsepower Norton engine, close-ratio five-speed gear box and disc brakes.

To justify any Dunstall bike, you need only love fast riding. Then you can do no better than a machine from Paul Dunstall.

## GARELLI (*See Chart #12*)

There have been no changes this year. Garelli still makes three machines with no serious failings. Theirs is a line you can trust.

Many part-time trail riders are looking for a machine light enough to carry in the trunk of a car yet versatile enough to take into the woods. The Gypsy is just such a machine.

## GREEVES (*See Chart #13*)

Greeves, too, is continuing with last year's designs—great competition bikes that have kept pace with the best for a number of years. The firm dropped the traditional I-beam frame last year in favor of a single downtube aluminum design. Into this bike Greeves has now put an engine with modifications for '71 which have increased the horsepower substantially.

The handling characteristics of all bikes have been consistently superb. The suspension systems are similar to those proven in 1970. Their two essentially equal machines have continued to demonstrate their abilities at events in Europe and America.

## HARLEY-DAVIDSON (*See Chart #14*)

The firm is one of the oldest manufacturers of motorcycles in the world and has managed to stay on top through depressions and wars by selling large numbers of respectable machines to police, the armed forces and big-cycle devotees. Their image has always been one of solid, American respectability.

But when the Japanese invaded the U.S. market with small cc bikes the masculine growl of the Sportster and Electra-Glide was not exactly what the buyer wanted. Harley's bright image faded.

Now the firm has a long line of bikes that include tempting small cycles as well as jet-hot big ones. The small-bike fancier can find exactly what he wants. But on the other hand, times bring change and the second-time buyer is now looking for something larger and more sophisticated. Harley has those bikes in spades. Whether you want a small cycle or a large one Harley has it this year. Seventy-one just has to be one of the firm's best years.

The Baja is Harley's serious dirt-racing threat. It was unveiled in the spring of 1970 at the Greenhorn Enduro—which it won handily. The bike still has all of the ingredients of a winner: Ceriani forks, single downtube frame, long wheelbase, 11.5 inches of ground clearance and only 212 pounds of weight.

When the firm entered the super-bike race with its Sportster XLCH, it was not so much a matter of creating a new machine—the XLCH had already been in production—as it was a matter of building a field around the bike. The move gave Harley an edge and they spent that time on a super-super bike.

This is the first year for the Super Glide and perhaps as it was developed the design thinking went something like this: What the market really needs is a cycle with personality, pizzaz and excitement. What buyers really want is a cycle with size (62.75-inch wheelbase), styling (a sleek tank and molded, layered seat) and color (electric red, white and blue). The answer is the super-super bike—the Super Glide.

## HODAKA *(See Chart #15)*

Both of Hodaka's machines are junior-sized giants in the racing field. They are based on an old Ace 90, first punched out to 100cc's, then split to become two models.

The basic equipment common to both is: a 98cc single cylinder two-stroke engine, a double downtube frame and similar suspension front and rear. The enduro is less competition-oriented and better equipped for the pleasure rider who has the experience to appreciate its racing heritage. The B is light (138 pounds), high (11.2 inches of ground clearance), and street legal (with full lighting). For the trail it can be fitted with a muffler and spark arrestor, and can be well shod with good trials universal rubber, 19 inches in front, 18 in the rear.

The motocross model is fondly called the Super Rat. Its builders call it Super, its competitors call it Rat and in the 100cc class the Hodaka has no superiors. It has wide tires for soft dirt traction, plenty of power, very little weight (about 170 pounds) and a quick-shift five-speed transmission: a difficult combination to beat.

## HONDA *(See Chart #16)*

Honda is the bike and the idea that lifted motorcycling to the level it enjoys today. The firm did it first by rebuilding the motorcycle image, then by emphasizing small bikes and finally by building equipment that was economical and reliable. The early models—the 50, 305 and 250—became the most sought-after of all machines partially because they were inexpensive but more because they had class and style.

Honda has never lost its hold on the import market. On one hand their 750 four-cylinder has successfully taken a slice from the big bike field and, on the other, their medium-sized two strokes have held a strong position in dirt racing.

The new bikes have excellent frames, transmissions and suspension systems. Their engines aren't just de-tuned street versions; they're power plants whose components and tuning have been directed at dirt riding. The only problem Honda seems to have (and it can be overcome) is weight.

## HUSQVARNA *(See Chart #17)*

The name Husqvarna conjures up the picture of the undisputed king of motocross competition. The two are one—and as long as Husky continues in its present successful designs, they should remain so.

The 400, Husky's newest machine, will be introduced later this season. The factory still hasn't released horsepower statistics, but when their 250cc plant puts out 32 horses, what will the 400 do? Put an engine like that in a frame renowned for its handling and limit the weight to 235 pounds and you've got a sure winner. That's what Husqvarna is doing.

## INDIAN *(See Chart #18)*

Floyd Clymer, a veteran of American motorcycling, revived the Indian name a couple of years ago in an effort to breathe life into a once-famous line of cycles.

Clymer died last year and all that remains are two mini-cycles and a 100cc scrambler.

## JAWA *(See Chart #19)*

The only Czech import on the U.S. scene is known for its winning record. The main factory rider, Joel Roberts, is a man with many European championships, gathered mainly on Jawas. He's a rider with the qualifications to ride for anyone, yet he stays with Jawa—not out of loyalty alone, but because the firm consistently makes fast bikes.

The 360 Motocross is a prime example. A high displacement two-stroke, it handles superbly, the weight distribution is ideal, and everything is right from tires to paint. It could be that somewhere within the line of motocross and enduro bikes there is one just right for you.

## KAWASAKI *(See Chart #20)*

Kawasaki is one of Japan's largest diversified manufacturers. Much of their technological emphasis has been on the development of aircraft, and when they decided to direct some of their engineering know-how to motorcycles, it was done with the care they give to supersonic planes. The result is a line of superb bikes that are faster and better than most.

Several of their machines are noteworthy. The first: their series of enduros. The Bighorn is typical. Its frame is a winning double downtube design with Kawasaki's famous Hatta forks in front and 5-way adjustable rear shocks. The engine is protected by a bash plate, the exhaust pipe is neatly upswept and the fenders are properly high to protect against the threat of mud packing in the woods.

The engine has Kawasaki's famous rotary valve design and 33 bursting horses. The lights are removable for scrambling and a factory hop-up kit can boost the horsepower to 45.

Mach III is Kawasaki's big one, a 3-cylinder stormer that, at 500cc's, holds the NHRA record of fastest production motorcycle in the quarter mile. It sells for one dollar under the thousand mark.

## MAICO *(See Chart #21)*

Maico is the maker of a complete line of terrifyingly fast motocross machines. Changes for '71 have included dropping the 125cc enduro, upping the 360cc motocross and enduro bikes to 400cc's, and adding a 501cc motocross bike.

The 250 is exactly the same as the competition machine that claimed the '69 victory in the German Grand Prix. What does it take to win? Maico's answer is 220 pounds, 38 horses, and handling that keeps it on the ground.

Their 501 is so new that not too much is known about it at this writing. It does have horses to spare, 8.5 inches of clearance and the outward appearance all the winning machines from Maico have.

## MB *(See Chart #22)*

The two cycles from MB are high quality competition models which deserve consideration by prospective buyers. The enduro is adaptable, right for riders who want a small, capable off-highway machine. It is obedient for trail and packing use and comes with a four-speed transmission and 10.75 inches of clearance. Who could ask for more?

## MONTESA *(See Chart #23)*

One of the oldest names in Spanish cycling, Montesa was the first home for Señor Bulto. He left because Montesa wouldn't put enough emphasis on competition.

Bulto should have waited: the firm is no longer guilty of that oversight. Montesa now builds some of the finest competition equipment on the Continent.

My favorite is the Cota, more because I like that kind of machinery than because it is better than others in the lineup. A high-powered competition machine, it has a wide range of power. The range is nice to have and I discovered that the power band would not be broader with detuning. That's good to know.

Another popular model is the King Scorpion. It competes in the crowded field of 250cc enduros—and looks extremely good. The bike has telescopic front forks (with plenty of travel) and a good power-to-weight ratio. You'll like it in the woods.

## MOTO GUZZI *(See Chart #24)*

Moto Guzzi has dropped their two smaller bikes this season, building only the 750cc Ambassador. We can't blame them for knowing they have a winner in the Ambassador. The bike is the equal of all other tourers. It is heavy at 560 pounds, but once the bike is rolling, weight doesn't seem to matter. The 60 horses drive the bike through a unique driveshaft.

To be a Moto Guzzi rider you must like touring and if you do the bike is right for you. When others have overheated or fouled their plugs or even vibrated apart, you can keep on going. The Ambassador is that kind of easy-riding, reliable machine.

## NORTON *(See Chart #25)*

Norton is one of the most venerable names in big-time cycling. It is true their dirt machines were slain in the two-stroke takeover that occurred several years ago, but in the field of high-quality British bikes Norton is still very much in the running.

The company still retains the name "scrambler" for

some bikes, but when the smallest is a street-equipped 750, it may be hard to take the machine as a serious threat. But don't count them short. On the street Nortons are another story and the Commando has to rate near the top of the pack. It has a strong engine, good suspension and the famous featherbed frame—an engineering combination that makes it jet-hot right out of the dealer's showroom. You could do worse than to own a cycle which will do zero to sixty in 4.8 seconds.

## OSSA (*See Chart #26*)

A relative newcomer, Ossa has a line of two-stroke singles that are difficult to beat. Seventy-one finds the firm in good shape with several cycles that could begin racking up dirt-track victories.

One is the 250cc motocross in their Stiletto line. The machine is a terror on the track and many riders like it for general off-highway riding because it becomes tractable in the boonies. But we recommend the Pioneer, an enduro designed for general street and trail use. It is a fast, handsome machine. Try the Plonker, too. It is a bike built for people who like to go many places with a high regard for their own comfort and safety—and it is a great out-of-the-crate trail machine.

## PENTON (*See Chart #27*)

John Penton is a racer with a reputation for winning. He took that reputation and all of his racing know-how and put them on the line behind a selection of lightweight, small displacement enduro and 'cross bikes. The result has been a string of wins for people riding Pentons and a new line of internationally respected cycles.

The Berkshire is the only holdover from last year's market; the rest are new or radically changed.

For the Berkshire, Penton has put Ceriani front forks

on a double downtube cradle frame and followed up with Ceriani shocks. The controls are Magura, and insures that the clutch works for all five close-ratio gears. The engine, made by Sachs, is protected by a sturdy bash plate drilled for lightness.

## PUCH (*See Chart #28*)

Another entry into the field of lightweight speed, and a good one at that. The Puch machines are engineered for racing; buy one if you want to race.

I prefer the 175 because it carries my weight better. It has Magura controls, Girling rear suspension, Ceriani front forks, tuned expansion chamber, Bosch electrics and a number of other features which add up to a very, very good machine.

## RICKMAN-METISSE (*See Chart #29*)

R-M began by first making parts and then chassis for middle-range (450cc) cycle engines that once came in machines too heavy to be considered trailworthy. They expanded to include Honda road engines and now make kits and chassis for everything from 100 to 750cc's.

In 1971 Rickman-Metisse has begun to build the whole cycle. They buy Hodaka 100B and Zundapp 125 engines and mount them into their own frames. The result is a unique bike. The frame is a double downtube cradle with Ceriani shocks, front Ceriani fork and Magura controls. Fenders are bright blue fiberglass as is the one-piece tank. The ground clearance is 9.5 inches and the two bikes each weigh less than 200 pounds.

## ROYAL ENFIELD

Shed a tear! For the Old British Standard! The Enfield is no longer shipped to the States. It is sad, but cheer—you can still order a frame for an Enfield engine from Rickman-Metisse. Order through Steens.

## SACHS *(See Chart #30)*

Sachs starts with a basic engine and hops it up for the enduro and cross-country, then hops it more for the motocross. This is the sort of sensible approach one expects from the German mind and Sachs cycles prove it works. The bikes are fast and reliable.

All three machines run Earles-type leading link front forks. The design is old and Sachs is the last holdout, but from the racing results it's safe to say the firm will hold onto the design for some time. The frame is a single downtube modified cradle and the engine has the widest sunburst fins in the industry. The machines are setting trends in small displacement racing and are well worth considering.

## SUZUKI *(See Chart #31)*

Suzuki is another Japanese builder who makes a bike for every purpose. As is the case with the others from the Orient, every model is good and the choice depends strictly on your tastes.

It is worth noting that Suzuki did extremely well last season racing in the dirt and now offers a 400cc competition machine. The cycle shows all of Suzuki's track-proven efforts and is a boomer.

The Cyclone is a spartan machine with few frills and much down-to-business equipment. The frame is new, a single downtube cradle with telescopic dampened forks and adjustable shocks aft. The engine puts out 40 horsepower and the full cycle weighs 236 pounds. With a five-speed transmission and a well-designed expansion chamber exhaust system, it is a bike you should see.

If you prefer street bikes, Suzuki makes three that

are especially good: the Hustler is a 250cc version, the Rebel a 350cc model and the Titan a 500cc super-bike.

## TRIUMPH (See Chart #32)

Despite the well-publicized two-stroke "domination" of dirt racing, the winning ways of Triumph have slowed but slightly. The bike still has a firm hold on road, flat track, short track, mile, half mile and other forms of racing.

Since BSA purchased Triumph, the two machines have shared research and development. That may be one reason why the Trident bears such a resemblance to the BSA Rocket 3. The 1971 street and enduro 250's are similar. If you don't believe us compare the statistics. But similarities aside, the machines have original ideas with individual, unique features. One notable example is Triumph's removable lighting. For dirt racing you simply unplug. There is no faster conversion.

Probably the best-known model now is the fire-breathing three, the Trident. Yet the firm's most important cycle, the bike on which its reputation was made, is the 650. It is a Tiger, literally, and the TR 6R is selling like furred fury.

The Tiger is a beautiful street machine with the power of a super-bike and the weight of a racer. It weighs only 380 pounds. It is surprisingly reliable: starts the first time and runs for thousands of miles with a smoothness you may expect only from a touring machine. The bike is exciting, well styled and well painted with an engine that roars music to stir the soul.

## VELOCETTE (See Chart #33)

The new Velocette is bred from road racing stock developed in another era. On one hand the current models seem to be pseudo-racers with big tanks; on the other hand the lean muscular look suggests they could be raced with very little alteration. Perhaps it is so, but the machines are equipped with full lighting systems and other important equipment for street and city driving. Yet racing considerations aside, if you are looking for a 500cc street rig, the Velocette has no peer.

## YAMAHA *(See Chart #34)*

Yamaha has run the gamut—from championship road racers to competitive single cylinder 2-stroke scramblers. All machines are offered to the public: two out-of-the-crate racers that can blow anything off the track except another Yamaha, three scramblers with as much power and maneuverability as anything built and a number of very good street and enduro bikes that will appeal to the noncompetitor rider.

To recount Yamaha road racing wins would be an endless chore. They've been undisputed champions for years. But it is important to remember that their winning ways often find an end in the best street machinery. The DT-1 is an example. It was the first attempt to replace a street/scrambler with an enduro version. The machine caught on and is probably the most successful trend-setter in the cycle world. Now virtually every builder has an enduro in his line.

The newest bike in the stable is the XS1-B, Yamaha's first four-stroke. The result is surprising. The bike has high speed (115mph), power throughout the range, and the road-feel of larger tourers. Yet the light, agile maneuverability it delivers somehow brings to mind the café racers of Britain.

## YANKEE *(See Chart #35)*

What's a Yankee? An Ossa engine in a competitive frame designed especially for fast riding by Yankee engineers. The idea is strictly competition. Used that way a Yankee can run hard against anything on the road.

The bikes have been used in a few small races during experimental periods and have scooped all comers without trouble. As yet the bikes are not in production, but the tentative schedule says you can buy them about the first of April. If you can, take a look.

## ZUNDAPP *(See Chart #36)*

Zundapp closes the alphabetical listing with four fine bikes that compete in the small-displacement classes. Two are street and trail models and the others are enduro machines. The 100cc version is the winner of many events, including the tough Greenhorn Enduro, which is notorious for destroying motorcycles. The bike comes with a heavy-duty frame, and an 18-inch wheel in the rear and a 21-inch forward for better control. Zundapp may be last in these listings, but in the field it often comes in first.

## Chart #1

AJS Norton Villers Corp., 6765 Paramount Blvd., Long Beach, Calif.

| Name | Type | Engine | No. of Cyl. | Displacement | Horsepower | Other |
|---|---|---|---|---|---|---|
| Stormer Y/40 | scrambler | 2-stroke | single | 250cc's | 28hp | 4-sp. trans. |
| Stormer Y/50 | scrambler | 2-stroke | single | 370cc's | 33hp | 4-sp. trans. |

## Chart #2

AMERICAN EAGLE
DISCONTINUED

## Chart #3

AUGUSTA Ed LaBelle Cycle Engineering, P.O. Box 322, Secane, Penn.

| Name | Type | Engine | No. of Cyl. | Displacement | Horsepower | Other |
|---|---|---|---|---|---|---|
| 125 S | street | 4-stroke | single | 125cc's | 9.5hp | 70mph |
| 125 GT | street-road racer | same as above with road racing seat and tank. | | | | |
| 250 | street | 4-stroke | twin | 247cc's | 18hp | 93mph |
| 250 S | enduro | same as above with solo seat and game rack. | | | | |
| MV-4 | street | 4-stroke | 4 | 590cc's | 52bhp | 118mph |
| Augusta | street-tourer | 4-stroke | 4 | 750cc's | 76bhp | 140mph |

## Chart #4

### BMW Flanders Company, 3405 Fair Oaks Avenue, Pasadena, Calif.

| Name | Type | Engine | No. of Cyl. | Displacement | Horsepower | Other |
|------|------|--------|-------------|--------------|------------|-------|
| R-50 | street | 4-stroke | twin | 490cc's | 36bhp | 98mph |
| R-60 | street | 4-stroke | twin | 590cc's | 46bhp | 105mph |
| R-75 | street | 4-stroke | twin | 745cc's | 57bhp | 115mph |

## Chart #5

### BENELLI Cosmopolitan Motors, Jacksonville and Meadowbrook Roads, Hatboro, Penn.

| Name | Type | Engine | No. of Cyl. | Displacement | Horsepower | Other |
|------|------|--------|-------------|--------------|------------|-------|
| Cougar | enduro | 2-stroke | single | 49cc's | n.a. (bhp) | 58mph |
| Sprite | street | 4-stroke | single | 125cc's | 11bhp | 60mph |
| Cobra | enduro | 2-stroke | single | 125cc's | 11bhp | 60mph |
| Sprite | street | 4-stroke | single | 200cc's | 15.5bhp | 70mph |
| Supersport | enduro | 4-stroke | single | 248cc's | 30bhp | 100mph |
| Tornado | street | 4-stroke | twin | 643cc's | 50bhp | 118mph |

## Chart #6

BRIDGESTONE Rockford Motors, 191 Harrison Ave., Rockford, Ill.

| Name | Type | Engine | No. of Cyl. | Displacement | Horsepower | Other |
| --- | --- | --- | --- | --- | --- | --- |
| 100 GP | street | 2-stroke | single | 99cc's | 11bhp | 65mph |
| 100 TMX | street | 2-stroke | single | 99cc's | 11bhp | 45mph |
| 200M II RS | street | 2-stroke | twin | 199cc's | 22bhp | 90mph |
| 200M IISS | street | 2-stroke | twin | 199cc's | 22bhp | 85mph |
| 350 GTR | street | 2-stroke | twin | 349cc's | 40bhp | 100mph |
| 350 GTO | street | 2-stroke | twin | 349cc's | 40bhp | 100mph |

## Chart #7

BSA BSA, West, P.O. Box 337, Duarte, Calif.

| Name | Type | Engine | No. of Cyl. | Displacement | Horsepower | Other |
| --- | --- | --- | --- | --- | --- | --- |
| Gold Star 250-SS | street/trail | 4-stroke | single | 250cc's | 22.5bhp | 290 pounds |
| Victor 250 Trail | enduro | 4-stroke | single | 250cc's | 22.5bhp | 287 pounds |
| Fury 350 | Street | 4-stroke | single | 350cc | 34bhp | 345 pounds |
| Fury 350SS | Street/Trail | 4-stroke | single | 350cc | 34bhp | 345 pounds |
| Gold Star 500-SS | street/trail | 4-stroke | single | 500cc's | 34bhp | 310 pounds |
| Victor 500-Trail | enduro | 4-stroke | single | 500cc's | 34bhp | 298 pounds |
| Victor 500-MX | motocross | 4-stroke | single | 500cc's | 38bhp | 240 pounds |
| Thunderbolt | street | 4-stroke | twin | 650cc's | 42bhp | 100 mph |
| Lightning | street | 4-stroke | twin | 650cc's | 45bhp | 100 mph |
| Firebird | street | 4-stroke | twin | 650cc's | 46bhp | 105 mph |
| Rocket 3 | street | 4-stroke | 3 | 750cc's | 60bhp | 127 mph |

*Chart #8*

**BULTACO Cemoto East Importing Co., 2040 Maxon Road, Schenectady, N. Y.**

| Name | Type | Engine | No. of Cyl. | Displacement | Horsepower | Other |
|---|---|---|---|---|---|---|
| Lobito | enduro | 2-stroke | single | 99cc's | 10hp | 5-sp. trans. |
| Lobito | enduro | 2-stroke | single | 124cc's | 12bhp | 5-sp. trans. |
| Campera | enduro | 2-stroke | single | 174cc's | 14bhp | 5-sp. trans. |
| Sherpa S 100 | scrambler | 2-stroke | single | 99cc's | 16.3bhp | 5-sp. trans. |
| Sherpa S 125 | scrambler | 2-stroke | single | 124cc's | 22bhp | 5-sp. trans. |
| Sherpa S 174 | scrambler | 2-stroke | single | 174cc's | 27bhp | 5-sp. trans. |
| Sherpa S 200 | scrambler | 2-stroke | single | 196cc's | 29bhp | 5-sp. trans. |
| El Tigre | enduro | 2-stroke | single | 196cc's | 20bhp | 80mph |
| Mercurio | street | 2-stroke | single | 196cc's | 20bhp | 80mph |
| Metralla | street | 2-stroke | single | 244cc's | 27.5bhp | 103mph (kit) |
| El Tigre | enduro | 2-stroke | single | 244cc's | 27.6bhp | 38bhp (kit) |
| Matador | enduro | 2-stroke | single | 244cc's | 22bhp | 70mph |
| Pursang Europa | motocross | 2-stroke | single | 244cc's | 35bhp | 5-sp. trans. |
| Pursang TT | scrambler | 2-stroke | single | 244cc's | 35bhp | 5-sp. trans. |
| Sherpa T | trials | 2-stroke | single | 244cc's | 20bhp | 5-sp. trans. |
| El Montadera | enduro | 2-stroke | single | 362cc's | 32.6bhp | 86mph |
| El Bandido | scrambler | 2-stroke | single | 362cc's | 43bhp | 4-sp. trans. |

## Chart #9

### CIMATTI American Cimatti, 3805 Jefferson, Houston, Texas

| Name | Type | Engine | No. of Cyl. | Displacement | Horsepower | Other |
|------|------|--------|-------------|--------------|------------|-------|
| Chic | moped | 2-stroke | single | 49cc's | 1.27bhp | 1-sp. trans. |
| Sport | road | 2-stroke | single | 49cc's | 6bhp | 5-sp. trans. |
| Cross | enduro | 2-stroke | single | 49cc's | 5bhp | 4-sp. trans. |
| Cross Competizione | motocross | 2-stroke | single | 49cc's | 7.5bhp | 6-sp. trans. |
| Sport Lusso | street | 2-stroke | single | 100cc's | 7.5bhp | 4-sp. trans. |
| Motocross | motocross | 2-stroke | single | 125cc's | 17.5bhp | 6-sp. trans. |
| Moto-Morini | enduro | 4-stroke | single | 125cc's | 16bhp | 5-sp. trans. |
| Sport Luzzo | street | 2-stroke | single | 175cc's | 12.5bhp | 4-sp. trans. |
| Moto Morini | enduro | 4-stroke | single | 175cc's | 20bhp | 5-sp. trans. |
| Cross Competizione | motox | 2-stroke | single | 175cc's | 19.5bhp | 4-sp. trans. |

## Chart #10

### DUCATI Berliner Motor Corp., Railroad St. and Plant Road, Hasbrouck Heights, N. J.

| Name | Type | Engine | No. of Cyl. | Displacement | Horsepower | Other |
|------|------|--------|-------------|--------------|------------|-------|
| 250 Mark 3D | street | 4-stroke | single | 250cc's | 22bhp | 5-sp. trans. |
| 350 Mark 3D | street | 4-stroke | single | 350cc's | 31bhp | 5-sp. trans. |
| 450 Mark 3D | street | 4-stroke | single | 450cc's | n.a. | 5-sp. trans. |
| 250 Scrambler | enduro | 4-stroke | single | 250cc's | 20bhp | 5-sp. trans. |
| 350 Scrambler | enduro | 4-stroke | single | 350cc's | 28bhp | 5-sp. trans. |
| 450 Jupiter | enduro | 4-stroke | single | 450cc's | n.a. | 5-sp. trans. |

## Chart #11

### DUNSTALL Paul Dunstall Equipment, 156 Well Hall Road, London, SE9, England

| Name | Type | Engine | No. of Cyl. | Displacement | Horsepower | Other |
|------|------|--------|-------------|--------------|------------|-------|
| Triumph Sprint | street | 4-stroke | twin | 744cc's | 128bhp | 4-sp. trans. |
| Triumph Export | street | 4-stroke | twin | 744cc's | 128bhp | 4-sp. trans. |
| Norton Tourer | tourer | 4-stroke | twin | 745cc's | 133bhp | 6-sp. trans. |
| Norton Sprint | street | 4-stroke | twin | 745cc's | 133bhp | 6-sp. trans. |
| Norton Export | street | 4-stroke | twin | 745cc's | 133bhp | 6-sp. trans. |

## Chart #12

### GARELLI American Rex, 1216 Monte Diablo Ave., San Mateo, Calif.

| Name | Type | Engine | No. of Cyl. | Displacement | Horsepower | Other |
|------|------|--------|-------------|--------------|------------|-------|
| Gypsy | street | 2-stroke | single | 97cc's | 11bhp | 60mph |
| Gran Premio | street | 2-stroke | single | 123cc's | (n.a.) bhp | 70mph |
| Gladiator | street | 2-stroke | single | 148cc's | 18.6bhp | 80mph |

## Chart #13

### GREEVES Nick Nicholson Motors, 11573 Van Owen, North Hollywood, Calif.

| Name | Type | Engine | No. of Cyl. | Displacement | Horsepower | Other |
|------|------|--------|-------------|--------------|------------|-------|
| Griffon | motocross | 2-stroke | single | 250cc's | 28.5bhp | 4-sp. trans. |
| Griffon | motocross | 2-stroke | single | 350cc's | 39bhp | 4-sp. trans. |

*Chart #14*

## HARLEY-DAVIDSON Harley-Davidson, 3700 West Jumeau Ave., Milwaukee, Wis.

| Name | Type | Engine | No. of Cyl. | Displacement | Horsepower | Other |
|------|------|--------|-------------|--------------|------------|-------|
| Leggero | street | 2-stroke | single | 65cc's | 4.9bhp | 65mph |
| Baja | scrambler | 2-stroke | single | 98cc's | (n.a.) bhp | 5-sp. trans. |
| Rapido | enduro | 2-stroke | single | 123cc's | 70bhp | 4-sp. trans. |
| Sprint SS | street | 4-stroke | single | 344cc's | 25bhp | 4-sp. trans. |
| Spring ERS | scrambler | 4-stroke | single | 344cc's | (n.a.) bhp | 4-sp. trans. |
| Sportster XLH | street | 4-stroke | twin | 883cc's | 58bhp | 115mph |
| Sportster XLCH | street | 4-stroke | twin | 883cc's | 68bhp | 120mph |
| Electra Glide FLP | street tourer | 4-stroke | twin | 1200cc's | 57bhp | 4-sp. trans. |
| Electra Glide FLH | street tourer | 4-stroke | twin | 1200cc's | 66bhp | 4-sp. trans. |
| Super Glide | street | 4-stroke | twin | 1200cc's | 66bhp | 117mph |

*Chart #15*

## HODAKA Pabatco, Box 327, Athena, Oregon

| Name | Type | Engine | No. of Cyl. | Displacement | Horsepower | Other |
|------|------|--------|-------------|--------------|------------|-------|
| Ace 100 B | enduro | 2-stroke | single | 98cc's | 9.8bhp | 62mph |
| Ace 100 MX | motocross | 2-stroke | single | 98cc's | (n.a.) bhp | 5-sp. trans. |

*Chart #16*

HONDA American Honda Motor Co., Inc, 100 West Alondra, Gardena, Calif.

| Name | Type | Engine | No. of Cyl. | Displacement | Horsepower | Other |
|---|---|---|---|---|---|---|
| PC-50 | moped | 4-stroke | single | 49cc's | 1.75bhp | 28mph |
| CL-70 | street | 4-stroke | single | 72cc's | 4.9bhp | 47mph |
| CT-90K1 | trail | 4-stroke | single | 90cc's | 7bhp | 56mph |
| CB-100 | street | 4-stroke | single | 100cc's | 11bhp | 5-sp. trans. |
| CL-100 | street | same as above with high pipe | | | | |
| SL-100 | enduro | 4-stroke | single | 100cc's | 11.5bhp | 65mph |
| CL-175 | street | 4-stroke | twin | 174cc's | 20bhp | 80mph |
| CL-175K3 | enduro | 4-stroke | twin | 174cc's | 19bhp | 68mph |
| CB 350 | street | 4-stroke | twin | 325cc's | 36bhp | 106mph |
| CL-350 | street | 4-stroke | twin | 325cc's | 33bhp | 100mph |
| SL-350K1 | enduro | 4-stroke | twin | 325cc's | 33bhp | 85mph |
| CB 450K3 | street | 4-stroke | twin | 444cc's | 45bhp | 112mph |
| CL 350K3 | street | 4-stroke | twin | 444cc's | 43bhp | 106mph |
| 750 Four | street | 4-stroke | 4 | 736cc's | 67bhp | 131mph |

## Chart #17

### HUSQVARNA MED-International, 4790 Palm Ave., La Mesa, Calif.

| Name | Type | Engine | No. of Cyl. | Displacement | Horsepower | Other |
|---|---|---|---|---|---|---|
| 250 Motocross | motocross | 2-stroke | single | 244cc's | 32bhp | 70mph |
| 360 Sportsman | enduro | 2-stroke | single | 352cc's | 30bhp | 90mph |
| 360 Motocross | motocross | 2-stroke | single | 352cc's | 34bhp | 80mph |
| 400 Motocross | motocross | 2-stroke | single | 400cc's | (n.a.) bhp | 80mph |

## Chart #18

### INDIAN Box 20749, Pico Heights Station, Los Angeles, Calif.

| Name | Type | Engine | No. of Cyl. | Displacement | Horsepower | Other |
|---|---|---|---|---|---|---|
| Scrambler | scrambler | 2-stroke | single | 100cc's | (n.a.) bhp | 4-sp. trans. |

## Chart #19

### JAWA American Jawa Ltd., 3745 Overland Ave., Los Angeles, Calif.

| Name | Type | Engine | No. of Cyl. | Displacement | Horsepower | Other |
|---|---|---|---|---|---|---|
| Trail Boss | enduro | 2-stroke | single | 125cc's | (n.a.) bhp | 4-sp. trans. |
| Trail Boss | enduro | 2-stroke | single | 175cc's | 68bhp | 4-sp. trans. |
| Trail Boss | enduro | 2-stroke | single | 250cc's | 16bhp | 72mph |
| Motocross | motocross | 2-stroke | single | 250cc's | 29bhp | 4-sp. trans. |
| Motocross | motocross | 2-stroke | single | 360cc's | 36bhp | 4-sp. trans. |

*Chart #20*

## KAWASAKI Kawasaki Motors Corp., 1062 McGaw Ave., Santa Ana, Calif.

| Name | Type | Engine | No. of Cyl. | Displacement | Horsepower | Other |
|---|---|---|---|---|---|---|
| Bushmaster | street | 2-stroke | single | 89cc's | 10.5bhp | 70mph |
| Bushmaster | street | 2-stroke | single | 99cc's | 11.5bhp | 66mph |
| Trail Boss | enduro | 2-stroke | single | 99cc's | 11.5bhp | 66mph |
| Enduro | enduro | 2-stroke | single | 124.9cc's | 17.5bhp | 72mph |
| Enduro | enduro | 2-stroke | single | 174cc's | 21.5bhp | 80mph |
| Avenger S | street | 2-stroke | twin | 338cc's | 42bhp | 115mph |
| Avenger T | trail | 2-stroke | twin | 338cc's | 42bhp | 100mph |
| Samurai S | street | 2-stroke | twin | 250cc's | 31bhp | 105mph |
| Samurai T | trail | 2-stroke | twin | 250cc's | 31bhp | 90mph |
| Enduro | enduro | 2-stroke | single | 246.8cc's | 24.5bhp | 85mph |
| Bighorn | enduro | 2-stroke | single | 346cc's | 33bhp | 45bhp (kit) |
| Mach III | street | 2-stroke | 3 | 498cc's | 60bhp | 124mph |

## Chart #21

### MAICO Cooper Motors, 110 East Santa Anita Ave., Burbank, Calif.

| Name | Type | Engine | No. of Cyl. | Displacement | Horsepower | Other |
|---|---|---|---|---|---|---|
| Motocross | motocross | 2-stroke | single | 125cc's | 21bhp | 75mph |
| Motocross | motocross | 2-stroke | single | 250cc's | 38bhp | 4-sp. trans. |
| Motocross | motocross | 2-stroke | single | 400cc's | 43bhp | 95mph |
| Enduro | enduro | 2-stroke | single | 400cc's | 43bhp | 90mph |
| Motocross | motocross | 2-stroke | single | 501cc's | (n.a.) bhp | 4-sp. trans. |

## Chart #22

### MB M.B. Sportcycles, 311 E. Alexander Ave., Tacoma, Wash.

| Name | Type | Engine | No. of Cyl. | Displacement | Horsepower | Other |
|---|---|---|---|---|---|---|
| XC100 | scrambler | 2-stroke | single | 98cc's | 15bhp | 70mph |
| XTR100A | enduro | 2-stroke | single | 98cc's | 9bhp | 67mph |

*Chart #23*

MONTESA Montesa Motors, Inc., 3657 West Beverly Blvd., Los Angeles, Calif.

| Name | Type | Engine | No. of Cyl. | Displacement | Horsepower | Other |
|------|------|--------|-------------|--------------|------------|-------|
| King Scorpion | enduro | 2-stroke | single | 247cc's | 22.8bhp | 85mph |
| Cota | trials | 2-stroke | single | 247cc's | 23bhp | 50mph |
| Cappra 5 | scrambler | 2-stroke | single | 247cc's | 33bhp | 90mph |
| Cappra GP | motocross | 2-stroke | single | 247cc's | 33bhp | 75mph |
| Cappra GP | motocross | 2-stroke | single | 351cc's | 30bhp | 90mph |
| Cappra DS | scrambler | 2-stroke | single | 351.2cc's | 38.5bhp | 4-sp. trans. |
| Cappra Scrambler | scrambler | 2-stroke | single | 351.2cc's | 38.5bhp | 4-sp. trans. |

*Chart #24*

MOTO GUZZI Premier Motor Corp., P.O. Box 15, Leonia, N. J.

| Name | Type | Engine | No. of Cyl. | Displacement | Horsepower | Other |
|------|------|--------|-------------|--------------|------------|-------|
| Ambassador | tourer | 4-stroke | twin | 750cc's | 60bhp | 116mph |

## Chart #25

### NORTON Norton Villers Corp., 6765 Paramount Blvd., Long Beach, Calif.

| Name | Type | Engine | No. of Cyl. | Displacement | Horsepower | Other |
|------|------|--------|-------------|--------------|------------|-------|
| N15 CS Scrambler | street | 4-stroke | twin | 745cc's | 53bhp | 115mph |
| Ranger P-11 A | street | same as above with low pipes and featherbed frame | | | | |
| Atlas | street | 4-stroke | twin | 745cc's | 53bhp | 4-sp. trans. |
| Commando | street | 4-stroke | twin | 745cc's | 58bhp | 125mph |
| Commando S | same as commando with trail dress | | | | | 110mph |

## Chart #26

### OSSA Yankee Motor Corp., P.O. Box 36, Schenectady, N. Y.

| Name | Type | Engine | No. of Cyl. | Displacement | Horsepower | Other |
|------|------|--------|-------------|--------------|------------|-------|
| Stiletto | motocross | 2-stroke | single | 175cc's | 28bhp | 5-sp. trans. |
| Stiletto | motocross | 2-stroke | single | 250cc's | 32bhp | 5-sp. trans. |
| Stiletto TT | scrambler | 2-stroke | single | 250cc's | 34bhp | 5-sp. trans. |
| Pioneer | enduro | 2-stroke | single | 175cc's | 18bhp | 5-sp. trans. |
| Pioneer | enduro | 2-stroke | single | 250cc's | 21bhp | 5-sp. trans. |
| Plonker | trials | 2-stroke | single | 250cc's | 18bhp | 11" clearance |

*Chart #27*

PENTON Penton Imports, Amhurst, Ohio

| Name | Type | Engine | No. of Cyl. | Displacement | Horsepower | Other |
|------|------|--------|-------------|--------------|------------|-------|
| Berkshire | motocross | 2-stroke | single | 98cc's | 13bhp | 5-sp. trans. |
| Enduro | enduro | 2-stroke | single | 125cc's | 18bhp | 5-sp. trans. |
| Motocross | motocross | 2-stroke | single | 125cc's | 21bhp | 5-sp. trans. |
| Enduro | enduro | 2-stroke | single | 175cc's | 20bhp | 5-sp. trans. |
| Motocross | motocross | 2-stroke | single | 175cc's | 24bhp | 5-sp. trans. |

*Chart #28*

PUCH Puch Motors Corp., 9825 Mason Ave., Chatsworth, Calif.

| Name | Type | Engine | No. of Cyl. | Displacement | Horsepower | Other |
|------|------|--------|-------------|--------------|------------|-------|
| Motocross | motocross | 2-stroke | single | 125cc's | 17bhp | 62mph |
| Motocross | motocross | 2-stroke | single | 175cc's | 21.5bhp | 74mph |

*Chart #29*

RICKMAN-METISSE Steens, 1635 W. Valley Blvd., Alhambra, Calif.

| Name | Type | Engine | No. of Cyl. | Displacement | Horsepower | Other |
|------|------|--------|-------------|--------------|------------|-------|
| 100 Micro | scrambler | 2-stroke | single | 100cc's | 9.8bhp | 5-sp. trans. |
| 125 Micro | scrambler | 2-stroke | single | 125cc's | 15bhp | 5-sp. trans. |

## Chart #30

SACHS Sachs Hercules Distributing Co., 1812 Colorado Ave., Santa Monica, Calif.

| Name | Type | Engine | No. of Cyl. | Displacement | Horsepower | Other |
|---|---|---|---|---|---|---|
| Enduro | enduro | 2-stroke | single | 123cc's | 15.5bhp | 5-sp. trans. |
| Cross Country | cross country | 2-stroke | single | 123cc's | 15.5bhp | 5-sp. trans. |
| Motocross | motocross | 2-stroke | single | 123cc's | 18.3bhp | 5-sp. trans. |

## Chart #31

SUZUKI U.S. Suzuki Motor Corp., 13767 Freeway Drive, Santa Fe Springs, Calif.

| Name | Type | Engine | No. of Cyl. | Displacement | Horsepower | Other |
|---|---|---|---|---|---|---|
| Cutlass | street | 2-stroke | single | 50cc's | 4.5bhp | 40mph |
| Gaucho | enduro | 2-stroke | single | 50cc's | 4.9bhp | 55mph |
| Honcho | enduro | 2-stroke | single | 90cc's | 11bhp | 60mph |
| Blazer | enduro | 2-stroke | single | 90cc's | 11bhp | 60mph |
| Cat | enduro | 2-stroke | single | 120cc's | 12bhp | 60mph |
| Duster | enduro | 2-stroke | single | 125cc's | 13bhp | 65mph |
| Stinger | street | 2-stroke | twin | 125cc's | 15.1bhp | 70mph |
| Sierra | enduro | 2-stroke | single | 185cc's | 17.5bhp | 70mph |
| Hustler | street | 2-stroke | twin | 250cc's | 33bhp | 95mph |
| Savage | enduro | 2-stroke | single | 250cc's | 23bhp | 75mph |
| Rebel | street | 2-stroke | twin | 350cc's | 40bhp | 100mph |
| Cyclone | scrambler | 2-stroke | single | 400cc's | 40bhp | 5-sp. trans. |
| Titan | street | 2-stroke | twin | 500cc's | 47bhp | 110mph |

*Chart #32*

TRIUMPH Johnson Motors, Inc., P.O. Box 275, Duarte, Calif.

| Name | Type | Engine | No. of Cyl. | Displacement | Horsepower | Other |
|---|---|---|---|---|---|---|
| Blazer SS | street/trail | 4-stroke | single | 250cc's | 22.5bhp | 290 pounds |
| Trail Blazer | enduro | 4-stroke | single | 250cc's | 22.5bhp | 287 pounds |
| Daytona | street | 4-stroke | twin | 490cc's | 41bhp | 100mph |
| Trophy | street | 4-stroke | twin | 490cc's | 38bhp | 4-sp. trans. |
| Trophy 650 | street | 4-stroke | twin | 649cc's | 45bhp | 95mph |
| Tiger | street | 4-stroke | twin | 649cc's | 45bhp | 96mph |
| Bonneville | street | 4-stroke | twin | 649cc's | 52bhp | 112mph |
| Trident | street | 4-stroke | 3 | 747cc's | 60bhp | 118mph |

*Chart #33*

VELOCETTE Vehicles, Ltd., 11 Pomfret St., Providence, R. I.

| Name | Type | Engine | No. of Cyl. | Displacement | Horsepower | Other |
|---|---|---|---|---|---|---|
| MSS | street | 4-stroke | single | 499cc's | 27bhp | 80mph |
| Venom | street | 4-stroke | single | 499cc's | 34bhp | 95mph |
| Clubman | street | 4-stroke | single | 499cc's | 37hp | 100mph |
| Thruxton | street | 4-stroke | single | 499cc's | 41bhp | 109mph |
| Scrambler | street | 4-stroke | single | 499cc's | 39bhp | 95mph |
| Endurance | street | 4-stroke | single | 499cc's | 34bhp | 90mph |

*Chart #34*

## YAMAHA Yamaha International, P.O. Box 54540, Los Angeles, Calif.

| Name | Type | Engine | No. of Cyl. | Displacement | Horsepower | Other |
|------|------|--------|-------------|--------------|------------|-------|
| G 6S B | street | 2-stroke | single | 73cc's | 4.9hp | 50mph |
| HS1 B | street | 2-stroke | single | 89cc's | 4.9hp | 53mph |
| HT1 B | enduro | 2-stroke | single | 89cc's | 8.5bhp | 55mph |
| AT1 C | enduro | 2-stroke | single | 123cc's | 11.5bhp | 62mph |
| AT 1MX | scrambler | 2-stroke | single | 123cc's | 18bhp | 5-sp. trans. |
| CT 1C | enduro | 2-stroke | single | 171cc's | 15.6bhp | 65mph |
| CS3 B | street | 2-stroke | twin | 195cc's | 22bhp | 85mph |
| TD 2 | road racer | 2-stroke | twin | 246cc's | 44bhp | 140+mph |
| DT1 E | enduro | 2-stroke | single | 246cc's | 23bhp | 73mph |
| DT 1MX | scrambler | 2-stroke | single | 246cc's | 30bhp | 5-sp. trans. |
| TR-2 | road racer | 2-stroke | twin | 348cc's | 54bhp | 150+mph |
| R5 B | street | 2-stroke | twin | 347cc's | 36bhp | 100mph |
| RT1 B | enduro | 2-stroke | single | 351cc's | 30bhp | 78mph |
| TR 1MX | scrambler | 2-stroke | single | 351cc's | 36bhp | 5-sp. trans. |
| XS1 B | street | 4-stroke | twin | 653cc's | 53bhp | 115mph |

*Chart #35*

## YANKEE Yankee Motor Corp., P.O. Box 36, Schenectady, N.Y.

| Name | Type | Engine | No. of Cyl. | Displacement | Horsepower | Other |
|------|------|--------|-------------|--------------|------------|-------|
| ISDT | enduro | 2-stroke | twin | 500cc's | 38bhp | 6-sp. trans. |
| Motocross | motocross | 2-stroke | twin | 500cc's | 42bhp | 6-sp. trans. |

*Chart #36*

## ZUNDAPP McCormack International, P.O. Box 10910, Santa Ana, Calif.

| Name | Type | Engine | No. of Cyl. | Displacement | Horsepower | Other |
|------|------|--------|-------------|--------------|------------|-------|
| Classic | street | 2-stroke | single | 98cc's | 9bhp | 60mph |
| Scrambler | street | 2-stroke | single | 98cc's | 9bhp | 60mph |
| ISDT Replica | enduro | 2-stroke | single | 98cc's | 9.3bhp | 65mph |
| ISDT | enduro | 2-stroke | single | 125cc's | (n.a.) bhp | 5-sp. trans. |

Chapter 3

# HOT BIKES AND COMPETITION KITS

ALMOST EVERY MOTORCYCLE MANUFACTURER is involved in racing. Some field factory teams and others build bikes private owners modify. Either way it is a rule that comparable models must be made available to the public. *That* means duplicates of machines like Yamaha's record-holding racers are available to anyone with the cash on hand.

The bikes are—almost. In Yamaha's dealer catalog, for example, you can find two road racers, a 250cc machine exactly (or nearly) like the ones class champions Gary Nixon and Yvon Du Hamel ride, and a 350cc like the one that panics most racing 750's. The 250 is rated at 44bhp and can top 135mph and the 350 is rated at 54bhp and can hit 150mph. Neither machine is your run-of-the-mill street cycle. Also listed are competition Yamaha motocross and enduro versions. There is an asterisk beside some models which indicates that a GYT kit bolts on the necessary competition goodies. We've chosen Yamaha but most of the other manufacturers have similar equipment.

Are these machines really offered to the public? Yes and no. They are not for the average rider. He could neither handle nor maintain a racing bike and the result, at best, would be poor publicity. But the super bikes are available, through special arrangements, to competent, dedicated, interested racing riders.

If you ask your dealer about competition machines he may shake his head, but switch the subject to competition kits and he smiles. If the manufacturer does any racing at all chances are he offers one or more hop-up kits that turn some of his docile street rigs into competition-bred stormers. Honda is a good example. Their 750cc tourer took the country by storm last year, but some buyers wanted to race the big ones. The factory set about rectifying the situation. They assembled a racing kit and when the bike won the hottest race in the U.S., at Daytona, the kit was news. The Honda kit is typical of those put out by most manufacturers, so let's see what it includes.

Honda begins with heavy-duty primary and cam drive chains. Adds an external oil cooler to raise the lubrication system capacity to four quarts, and includes special pistons that raise the compression from 9:1 to 10.5:1. The new pistons have one compression and one oil ring. By comparison the stock version has three rings, two compression and one oil.

A new cylinder head is added with oversized intake valves and smaller exhaust valves. Special high tension springs are included to help raise the maximum rpm from 8500 to 10,500. A new cam opens the valves wider and longer, altering the timing for more power. New carburetors are added and a close-ratio transmission is coupled to the engine to make use of the narrow rpm range. Suspension and other components are also beefed up. The result is a 90 horsepower machine, 23 more than stock. Currently, this exciting kit is not available to the public.

Other bikes offer similar racing deals. BSA and Triumph are in road racing with strong, hot three's. Dealers throughout the country have been installing kits and cleaning up at local tracks. The three's—the

engines are similar since BSA owns both companies—
have an impressive list of records.

Also qualifying as a manufacturer is Paul Dunstall,
an English designer-racer-builder who takes Triumph
650's and Norton 750's and rebuilds them with his own
special parts. His alterations are so complete he is
recognized as a motorcycle manufacturer. His bikes are
called "Dunstall-Norton" or "Dunstall-Triumph" and
are sold in the U.S. through several outlets. They are
raced in A.M.A. events.

For the technically minded, 1971 improvements to
the Norton include:

> Re-sphered combustion chambers, 73mm instead
> of 68mm
> Steeper inlet valve angle, 26½° instead of 28°
> Larger inlet valves, 1⅝" in place of 1½"
> Larger inlet ports, 1¼" in place of 1¾₁₆"
> Inlet and exhaust ports reshaped and polished for
> maximum gas flow
> 10:1 compression in place of 9:1

In addition Dunstall will build a fantastic road racer
that can challenge nearly anything moving. Since 200
have not been produced, the rig isn't legal in AMA
events, but if it is flat-out speed and acceleration you
want, check this.

Dunstall is worth keeping in mind if you own a
Triumph or Norton. In addition to special cycles and
racing kits, he will sell parts and separate products.
Typical of these is the special Norton forks-brake.
After engineering a highly efficient hydraulic racing
fork, Dunstall casts a lower casing to include dual disc
brakes. The unit is lightweight and very, very efficient.

Bultaco is the father of dirt bikes. At the time
Japanese bikes were revolutionizing the motorcycle
image in the United States, Bultaco was experimenting
with large single-cylinder, two-stroke engines. At that

time the top dirt racers were running 500 and 650cc four-strokes. Bultaco stepped into the picture with its 250cc two-stroke engine and cleaned up, coming away with nearly every award.

Now the firm shares the field with other makes, but their dirt machines are still tops in competition. The only nondirt models Bultaco offers are the 200cc Mercurio and the 250cc Metralla (available with a factory racing kit). The El Tigre is a dual-purpose machine and the 250 is offered with competition equipment that increases its horses from 27 to 38.

Greeves is a smaller builder whose inclinations direct them toward dirt machines. It's possible that Bert Greeves wouldn't be happy building anything else. He makes two dirt machines that rank with the best. Harley-Davidson has racing cycles, as well. The best known is the Baja 100, winner of the Greenhorn Enduro during its first production year. Another model, perhaps less well publicized, is the Sprinter S, a 350cc four-stroke scrambler. Hodaka offers two machines. The first, the 100cc 100B, is a popular enduro bike. The other is the famous Super Rat, a machine many riders call the best 100cc scrambler in the business.

Husqvarna is the current king of motocross with four machines, a 250, two 360's and a 405cc model. Horsepower ranges from 32 to 34 and "unadvertised." The firm makes no racing kits: Husqvarna doesn't have to. Kawasaki makes several strong enduros, and a hot line of competition bikes called Greenstreaks. One is a 100cc version, the other a 250. Both are fast, quick-handling, winning bikes.

Maico offers six dirt runners. Two are enduros, four are motocross machines. Limited hop-up items are available from the factory and more are offered by specialty custom builders. For example, the stock front forks have external springs. A custom installation replaces them with internal springs for a better ride. Engine improvements include larger carburetor jets, porting and a tuned expansion chamber.

Consider Montesa next. The King Scorpion is too tame to be a good enduro machine, but the other bikes are all business: two 250cc's, a scrambler, a motocross machine and three 360's. Their 360GP is strictly a competition desert bike.

Ossa makes impressive dirt machines. You can choose from a variety of sizes in scrambler, enduro and trail models. The enduro version is the most outstanding.

Penton is named after its creator, John Penton, a veteran dirt racer. He makes great competition bikes, a 125cc scrambler, a 125 and 175cc ISDT. Penton's three sons took two gold medals and one silver medal at last year's Berkshire Trials.

Puch makes two lightweight machines (125cc). One is a very good motocross bike with a six-speed transmission, Ceriani forks and Magura controls. Rickman-Metisse makes two scramblers this year, a 100cc Hodaka-powered bike and the other a 125cc version with a Zundapp engine. The firm also makes scrambler frames for larger British bikes.

Suzuki competes in the European motocross circuit with a group of experimental bikes. Last year they were champions but the only bike to filter down to the U.S. thus far is a 400cc version. It is a real boomer.

Yamaha was the first Japanese manufacturer to offer an enduro in place of street scramblers. The firm now offers a GYT kit that makes its 250 and 360cc cycles tops in their class. If this kind of machinery is your bag, get in on the action and go GYT. Yankee is a beautiful machine with a 500cc Ossa two-stroke that puts out 35 horses for the enduro version and 42 in a scrambler model. The bikes have not caught on, but when they do you can bet Yankee will be one of the machines to beat. Zundapp makes ISDT cycles and ISDT winners. The 100cc Replica took two-in-a-row recently and is a threat wherever it races.

## THE FUTURE

In 1971, or perhaps 1972, you can look for half a dozen new, hot machines. They may be introduced as racing bikes or as street machines. Eventually they may be both. Now the information is strictly rumor—but rumor has it these are the big bikes you can look for.

**Honda**—Look for two machines. One will be a small but big-bore single. Honda needs a fast version to compete with other builders. Chances are good a 250 to 400cc model will be introduced soon, but some experts predict a 500cc model. In any case the engine will be of radical design, possibly with a magnesium block and four valves per cylinder.

The other bike will probably be a 500cc four. It could be a "smaller" version of the bike that made such a hit at the Tokyo Motor Show two years ago. The cycle may look like the 750 and it will be hot. It has to be to square off against Kawasaki's Mach III.

**Kawasaki**—It is rumor but . . . Competition is growing tougher in the big bike field and information continues to leak that Kawasaki has a super-secret 750 four in the works. We are told engineers are working on exotic ideas for the machine—electronic ignition, twin cams, fuel injection and a V-4 design. If the bike is introduced it will probably make its appearance one year from now.

Also be on the lookout for several new threes. The success of the Mach III has been so overwhelming Kawasaki wants to continue, perhaps with a 250, 350 or even a 650 version. If so, racing models are near at hand.

**Suzuki**—Reporters have long looked for a 750 bike from Suzuki and this may be the year. News has it that the engine will be water-cooled with 70bhp or more. The frame will probably feature some of the TR 500 design that handled so well. Those who have seen the prototype say the exhaust design is unique. The pipe splits into duals as on the BSA and Triumph.

Suzuki is the World's Motocross Champion and you can bet they will capitalize on that publicity. A 400cc single is probably first in line and you can be certain it will feature such refinements as electronic ignition.

**Yamaha**—What does the firm that has everything need most? Something to compare with the big bikes. There are rumors that the firm has a 800cc three-cylinder machine in development. There is no confirmation, but then a machine this hot wouldn't be leaked to the press until introduction time.

Chapter 4

# MINI-BIKE ROUNDUP:

## A Complete Listing of Mini-bikes and all Terrain Cycles

EVERYONE INVOLVED with motorcycling, no matter how remotely, is aware of the boom in mini-biking. Today so many buyers want the small machines it is difficult to keep production up to demand. Annual sales are running close to half a million and more is expected. Several motorcycle manufacturers have at least one mini-bike in their line and new manufacturers are joining the field.

Criticisms have been levelled at the mini's by thoughtless people who stepped from 250cc enduros to a four-horse Tecumseh-driven mini and found it lacking. But comparisons are misleading. Mini-bikes and motorcycles have two wheels and are motor-driven, but the similarity ends there. When you try them, the thrills and excitement is different: they are distinct machines.

Defining a mini-bike in terms of what it has is difficult. Models now marketed range from fully suspended, completely lighted, powerful machines to simple, unsuspended machines with pipe frames, lawn mower engines and garden tractor tires. Their characteristics vary just as much.

But the realm of the mini, the area in which it is obviously the best machine available, can be defined. Two

features mark the boundaries—lightness and compact-
ness. The mini-bike is small, lightweight and easy to
use by any rider from six to sixty. Reductions in size
and weight are achieved by using small components
(engines, frames, wheels and forks) and by eliminating
such heavy items as batteries, lights and sophisticated
engineering. Even suspension systems are generally
optional. The result is a super-lightweight rig capable
of carrying one passenger, small enough to be tucked
into the trunk of a car or tied to the back of a camper.
Its size makes it a machine young riders can handle
confidently.

But the design also limits its use. Minis are difficult to
see in traffic and are often unstable at highway speeds.
They are not the utilitarian machine a standard cycle
is and efforts to license them are unwise.

I had a chance to ride a Bonanza, one of the best
minis we've seen. It looks like a motorcycle in miniature
with telescopic front forks and surprisingly good rear
suspension. The frame has a double down tube cradle
and its engine is a 100cc two-stroke Hodaka single,
a power plant commonly found on full-sized bikes.
The model was scrambler-equipped for rough country
with an expansion chamber exhaust but no lights.

The performance was surprising. The bike carried me
up the side of a precariously steep hill with power to
spare, then left me at the top with the feeling that
riding skill alone wasn't the reason I'd made it. Later,
I found a deserted stretch of pavement and decided
to see if the 100cc mini-bike translated power into
top speed the way a full-sized 100cc motorcycle did.
The bike was fast, although geared low for the trail, but
I got the distinct impression the machine was not for
the road.

Although this speaks eloquently against using a mini

on the street, it is not an argument against the concept. On the contrary, mini-bikes are not only fun, but are also perfect training grounds for young, new riders. Many cities have, or are building, off-road riding areas and here a boy with a mini can develop a "motorcycle sense" that will remain with him throughout life.

According to statistics, most motorcycle accidents occur during the first hundred miles of riding. If a rider begins on the road, fighting street traffic, his early experiences will be frightening, hectic and dangerous. But if he begins off the road, in safe areas on a small bike he can handle, the danger is greatly reduced. Without pressure he can learn the controls and balance of a machine, can master turning and stopping, and when over-confidence sets in, as it always does, the mistakes will be of little consequence.

The newest wrinkle in small bikes is the "maxi-mini"—that is, a cycle somewhat larger than the conventional mini yet smaller and lighter than a standard machine. If you are one who dislikes the super-small wheels and reduced leg room of a regular mini, you will like the new size. The latest bikes have 15-inch wheels and many standard-bike features including big brakes and good leg room.

Several manufacturers offer them and more are on the way, but the best one I've seen yet is Yamaha's new Mini-Enduro. Yamaha executives told us they wanted something to "combat the flood of really small machines" and the Mini-Enduro is the answer. What an answer. The new bike stands 35½ inches high, is 62 inches long scales in at 121 pounds.—small enough to fit in any car, light enough to man-handle and good-looking enough to be proud of. Its 60cc rotary valve two-stroke is detuned to 4½ hp, power enough to push the bike along at 40mph. The ride is tremendous.

A friend of ours took the Mini-Enduro into the Los

Angeles mountains for a test recently. When he returned his eyes were wide with enthusiasm. He reported the bike could go any place a regular trail machine goes and could do anything his big cycle does. "Great things come in small packages," he commented.

## WHAT TO LOOK FOR

With the exception of a few larger machines like the Mini-Enduro, the rules that apply to motorcycle buying don't apply to mini-bikes at all. Instead of choosing a machine for street or trail, you buy a bike for its ride and handling. The only restriction is price. How do you find one? These guideposts should help.

Forget the "mini-choppers," cute copies of what can only be called a custom machine of questionable handling. In my opinion they are the poorest-designed, poorest-riding bikes offered. The attractive, exaggerated fork length makes the bike difficult to handle and is the machine's most vulnerable point, the first to break when confronted by a bumpy, rough trail. I've found most have poor balance with seating that only throws you further off balance when you hit the throttle. You like wheelies? This one will get you.

As for the other minis, the general rule is the more the machine looks like a regular motorcycle, the better it is. Check tires, suspension, frame, engine and other points.

*Tires*    An important item, as basic on a mini as on a full-scale bike. Less expensive machines may offer square-edged garden-tractor type tires. Question them. The tires are designed to be used vertically without the cornering common on cycles as you turn. The bike can be difficult to handle and the result may be spills that could be avoided with the rounded-profile tires.

Tire size, height and width are important. The taller the tire, the greater the stability it offers. Wide tires offer better traction than narrow ones—and better flotation on sand as well.

*Suspension*   Good springs make the ride softer and help to keep the wheels in contact with the ground. The right suspension offers more control.

The best front suspension is the telescopic-hydraulic leading link or Earles type, but only a handful of custom minis bother to offer it. (Incidentally, the Yamaha Mini-Enduro does.) On smaller minis your best bet is coiled spring suspension—it is especially recommended in the rear. Try the bike. Sit on it; see how your weight affects the springs. They should compress beneath your weight but if they draw too tightly the ride will suffer. If they compress too light, the ride will be hard.

*Frame*   Balance is important and too many mini-bikes put too much weight aft. Front control is minimal and wheelies are easy. Check weight distribution with care. The manufacturer should put as much weight forward as possible. The engine should be mounted between the wheels and the seat should be as far forward as leg room allows. Compare frame lengths: the longer the frame, the better the control.

While you are looking check the welds carefully. They show the care a manufacturer takes with his machine. If the welds are sloppy, minimal or cracked, be careful.

*Engine*   Your choice begins with two and four strokes and a poorly worded rule is this: A two-stroke with 50 to 100cc's is *always* a sign of quality BUT some very good machines offer four-stroke engines. In short, it is your choice.

Two-strokes develop a great deal of power but are harder on plugs and are fed a mixture of gas and oil that must be premixed. Four strokes are more reliable and have a better plug life and last longer, but deliver less kick. The differences are minimal.

The term "power requirement" is misunderstood by people used to full-sized cycles. The needs are different. Since the purpose of a mini is in off-road situations, great amouts of horsepower and top speed are meaningless. A mini with a good torque converter and a small engine can easily take a full-sized man over rough ground—anywhere he wants to go.

Some mini-bikes use a standard three- or four-speed transmission as a part of the engine package. Others use clutches or automatic devices. Some include a torque converter or the centrifugal clutches familiar on karts. Any of them will work, but the centrifugal clutch is not recommended for rugged use. Various sizes of chain are used, but #40 is probably best. Smaller chains are a source of trouble, derailing, breakage and kinking.

*Other equipment*    Brakes are important. Some manufacturers build mini-bikes without front brakes. Rears will work, but stopping distances are vastly improved with front brakes. We recommend them.

You won't need lighting if the bike is a sometimes machine, but if it will be used after dark, or if your favorite running area is shared with bikes of many sizes or other machines, dune buggies, four-wheel drives, ATVS, then insist on lights. A headlight during the day increases your safety.

Control positions are responsible in part for easy handling. If they are arranged oddly or backward, they may make the transition from mini-bike to motorcycle difficult. Buy a bike with controls as similar to a motorcycle as you can. A few minis have folding pegs, which improved riding in the rough and make storage easier. The brake and clutch levers should have ball ends for improved safety and should be made of a malleable metal that can be straightened after a fall.

## 1971 MINI-BIKES

| Name | Power | Eng. Type | Speed | Type |
|------|-------|-----------|-------|------|
| **ARCTIC CAT** | Arctic Ent., Thief River Falls, Minnesota | | | |
| SSS Cat | 4bhp | 2-cycle | 47cc's | mini-trail |
| | | | | |
| **BENELLI** | Cosmo Motors, Hatboro, Pennsylvania | | | |
| Compact | 7bhp | 2-cycle | 65cc's | mini-road |
| Trail | 7bhp | 2-cycle | 65cc's | mini-trail |
| Hornet | 3.5bhp | 2-cycle | 65cc's | mini-road |
| Buzzer | 3.5bhp | 2-cycle | 65cc's | mini-road |
| Volcano | 18bhp | 2-cycle | 180cc's | mini-motocross |
| | | | | |
| **BIRD ENGINEERING** | Box 427, DTS, Omaha, Nebraska | | | |
| Wren | 2.5bhp | 4-cycle | 25mph | mini-road |
| Lark | 3.5bhp | 4-cycle | 30mph | mini-road |
| Duck | 3.5bhp | 4-cycle | 25mph | mini-road |
| | | | | |
| **BONANZA** | Bonanza Inc., 1775 So. 1st St., San Jose, California | | | |
| 250 | 2.5bhp | 4-cycle | 25mph | mini-road |
| 300 | 3.5bhp | 4-cycle | 30mph | mini-road |
| BC 1100 | 3bhp | 4-cycle | 30mph | mini-road |
| BC 1200 | 3.5bhp | 4-cycle | 35mph | mini-road |
| BC 1300 | 4bhp | 4-cycle | 35mph | mini-trail |
| BC 1400T | 5bhp | 4-cycle | 40mph | mini-trail |
| BC 1500SH | 10bhp | 2-cycle | 55mph | mini-enduro |
| Mini-Moto | 11bhp | 2-cycle | 55mph | mini-motocross |
| Minichopper | 4bhp | 4-cycle | 35mph | mini-chopper |
| Minichopper | 10bhp | 2-cycle | 50mph | mini-chopper |

A new mid-cycle was introduced recently—100cc engine, five-speed transmission, 16-inch rims. Ceriani-type forks. The machine has set two World's Speed Records at Bonneville and taken the World Championship Open Class Mini-bike title.

| Name | Power | Eng. Type | Speed | Type |
|------|-------|-----------|-------|------|
| **BRONCO** | 2600 Bristol Pike, Cornwall Heights, Pa. | | | |
| T/X 1S | 3.8bhp | 4-cycle | 30mph | mini-road |
| T/X 1D | 3.8bhp | 4-cycle | 30mph | mini-trail |
| T/X 4 | 3bhp | 4-cycle | 25mph | mini-road |
| T/X 6 | 5bhp | 2-cycle | 55mph | mini-trail |
| T/X 7 | 4bhp | 2-cycle | 40mph | mini-trail |
| T/S 4 | 5bhp | 2-cycle | 55mph | mini-enduro |
| T/C 4 | 5bhp | 2-cycle | 55mph | mini-motocross |

| Name | Power | Eng. Type | Speed | Type |
|------|-------|-----------|-------|------|

**CHARGER** Central Cycle Supply, 51025 U.S. 31 North, South Bend, Indiana

| Name | Power | Eng. Type | Speed | Type |
|------|-------|-----------|-------|------|
| Junior | 3bhp | 4-cycle | 30mph | mini-road |
| I | 5bhp | 4-cycle | 35mph | mini-road |
| II | 3bhp | 4-cycle | 30mph | mini-road |
| III | 4bhp | 4-cycle | 35mph | mini-road |
| Trail Boss | 5bhp | 4-cycle | 35mph | mini-trail |
| Grasshopper | 4bhp | 4-cycle | 35mph | mini-chopper |

**EXPLORER** Thomas Co., 310 Franklin St., Clinton, Michigan

| Name | Power | Eng. Type | Speed | Type |
|------|-------|-----------|-------|------|
| Deluxe Trail | 5bhp | 4-cycle | 42mph | mini-trail |

**FOX** Fox Corp., Janesville, Wisconsin

| Name | Power | Eng. Type | Speed | Type |
|------|-------|-----------|-------|------|
| Sprite | 2.5bhp | 4-cycle | 25mph | mini-road |
| Spoiler | 4bhp | 4-cycle | 35mph | mini-trail |
| Condor | 4bhp | 4-cycle | 35mph | mini-road |
| Doodle Bug FX | 3bhp | 4-cycle | 35mph | mini-trail |
| Doodle Bug | 3.5bhp | 4-cycle | 35mph | mini-road |
| Trail Tramp | 4bhp | 4-cycle | 35mph | mini-trail |
| Trail FX | 4bhp | 4-cycle | 35mph | mini-trail |
| Street Scamp | 4bhp | 4-cycle | 35mph | mini-road |
| Campus FX | 4bhp | 4-cycle | 35mph | mini-road |

**HERTER'S** Herter's Incorporated, Dept. 1Y1, Waseca, Minnesota

| Name | Power | Eng. Type | Speed | Type |
|------|-------|-----------|-------|------|
| Mark 1 | 5bhp | 4-cycle | 35mph | mini-trail |

**HONDA** Honda Motor Co., 100 West Alondra Blvd., Gardena, Calif.

| Name | Power | Eng. Type | Speed | Type |
|------|-------|-----------|-------|------|
| Road 50 | 1.85bhp | 4-cycle | 20mph | mini-road |
| Trail 50 | 2bhp | 4-cycle | 28mph | mini-trail |
| Trail 70 | 5bhp | 4-cycle | 47mph | mini-trail |

**INDIAN** Indian, 1535 W. Rosecrans Ave., Gardena, California

| Name | Power | Eng. Type | Speed | Type |
|------|-------|-----------|-------|------|
| Minimini | n.a. | 2-cycle | 12mph | micro-mini |
| Boy Racer | 4.8bhp | 2-cycle | 50mph | mini-scrambler |
| Bobcat | 4.9bhp | 2-cycle | 50mph | mini-trail |
| Scrambler | 6.0bhp | 2-cycle | 60mph | mini-scrambler |

**KAWASAKI** Kawasaki Mtrs. Corp., 1062 McGaw Ave., Santa Ana, Cal.

| Name | Power | Eng. Type | Speed | Type |
|------|-------|-----------|-------|------|
| Coyote | 3bhp | 2-cycle | 25mph | mini-trail |
| Dyna Mite | 5bhp | 2-cycle | 40mph | mini-trail |

| Name | Power | Eng. Type | Speed | Type |
|------|-------|-----------|-------|------|
| **K-G   K-G Engineering, Box 71, Holliston, Massachusetts** | | | | |
| 350 T/C | 5bhp | 4-cycle | n.a. | mini-trail |
| | | | | |
| **MICHRINA   Michrina Ent., 14580 Fielding, Detroit, Michigan** | | | | |
| Blazer | 2.5bhp | 4-cycle | 15mph | mini-road |
| Outlaw I | 3bhp | 4-cycle | 30mph | mini-road |
| Outlaw II | 3bhp | 4-cycle | 30mph | mini-road |
| 450 | 3bhp | 4-cycle | 15mph | mini-trail |
| 500 | 3bhp | 4-cycle | 15mph | mini-trail |
| 600 | 3bhp | 4-cycle | 15mph | mini-trail |
| 700 | 4bhp | 4-cycle | 30mph | mini-trail |
| 4500 | 3bhp | 4-cycle | 25mph | mini-trail |
| 5000 | 3bhp | 4-cycle | 25mph | mini-trail |
| 6000 | 4bhp | 4-cycle | 35mph | mini-trail |
| 7000 | 4bhp | 4-cycle | 35mph | mini-trail |
| | | | | |
| **MONTGOMERY WARD, 619 W. Chicago Ave., Chicago, Illinois** | | | | |
| 323 | 3bhp | 4-cycle | 20mph | mini-trail |
| 424 | 3bhp | 4-cycle | 25mph | mini-trail |
| 424XE | 4bhp | 4-cycle | 25mph | mini-trail |
| 525 | 4bhp | 4-cycle | 30mph | mini-trail |
| 525XE | 4bhp | 4-cycle | 30mph | mini-trail |
| | | | | |
| **NOVA   Nova Prod. of California, 16800 S. Broadway, Gardena, Calif.** | | | | |
| Mustang | 2.5bhp | 4-cycle | 15mph | mini-road |
| Deluxe Sport | 3bhp | 4-cycle | 20mph | mini-trail |
| Super Sport | 4bhp | 4-cycle | 30mph | mini-road |
| Ruff Rider | 4.5bhp | 4-cycle | 40mph | mini-trail |
| King Cobra | 4bhp | 4-cycle | 35mph | mini-trail |
| Ruff Rider | 10bhp | 2-cycle | 60mph | mini-scrambler |
| | | | | |
| **J. C. PENNEY 1301 Ave. of the Americas, New York, New York** | | | | |
| Foremost | 2.5bhp | 4-cycle | 20mph | mini-road |
| Pinto | 3.5bhp | 4-cycle | 25mph | mini-road |
| El Tigre | 4.0bhp | 4-cycle | 25mph | mini-road |
| | | | | |
| **POWER DYNE 55 Tower St., Pawtucket, Rhode Island** | | | | |
| 1000 | 5bhp | 4-cycle | 45mph | mini-trail |
| | | | | |
| **PROJECTS UNLIMITED 1926 E. Siebenthaler Ave., Dayton, Ohio** | | | | |
| Skat Kitty | 2.5bhp | 4-cycle | 20mph | mini-sidecar |

| Name | Power | Eng. Type | Speed | Type |
|------|-------|-----------|-------|------|

### RUPP   Rupp Manufacturer, 1775 Airport Rd., Mansfield, Ohio

| Name | Power | Eng. Type | Speed | Type |
|------|-------|-----------|-------|------|
| Chopper | 2.5bhp | 4-cycle | 25mph | mini-road |
| Scrambler | 3.5bhp | 4-cycle | 30mph | mini-scrambler |
| Sprint | 3.5bhp | 4-cycle | 30mph | mini-trail |
| Enduro | 5bhp | 4-cycle | 35mph | mini-scrambler |
| Roadster | 5bhp | 4-cycle | 45mph | mini-road |

### RUTTMAN   Ruttman, 24732 Ford Road, Dearborn, Michigan

| Name | Power | Eng. Type | Speed | Type |
|------|-------|-----------|-------|------|
| Vulture | 3.5bhp | 4-cycle | 20mph | mini-road |
| Horny Toad | 3.5bhp | 4-cycle | 20mph | mini-trail |
| Grasshopper | 4bhp | 4-cycle | 25mph | mini-road |
| Wild Goose | 4bhp | 4-cycle | 25mph | mini-trail |
| Pack Mule | 4bhp | 4-cycle | 30mph | mini-trail |
| Pack Mule | 5bhp | 4-cycle | 35mph | mini-trail |

### SPORTSTYL  Box 94 Route 4, Lewistown, Pennsylvania

| Name | Power | Eng. Type | Speed | Type |
|------|-------|-----------|-------|------|
| Mouse | 2.5bhp | 4-cycle | 25mph | mini-road |
| Tom Kat | 2.5bhp | 4-cycle | 25mph | mini-trail |
| Super Mouse | 3.5bhp | 4-cycle | 30mph | mini-road |
| Tom Kat | 3.5bhp | 4-cycle | 30mph | mini-road |
| Dragon | 3.5bhp | 4-cycle | 30mph | mini-road |
| Alley Kat | 3.5bhp | 4-cycle | 25mph | mini-road |
| Kamp Kat | 5bhp | 4-cycle | 35mph | mini-trail |
| Alley Kat | 5bhp | 4-cycle | 35mph | mini-road |

### STELLER   Steller Electronics & Mfg. Corp., 131 Sunnyside Blvd., Plainview, New York

| Name | Power | Eng. Type | Speed | Type |
|------|-------|-----------|-------|------|
| Maxi-Super | top speed (n.a.) | 4-stroke engine | 5bhp | |

### SUZUKI   U.S. Suzuki Mtr. Corp., 13767 Freeway Dr., Santa Fe Springs, California

| Name | Power | Eng. Type | Speed | Type |
|------|-------|-----------|-------|------|
| Trail Hopper | 3bhp | 2-cycle | 35mph | mini-enduro |

### TACO Steens Inc., P.O. Box 2276, Alhambra, California

| Name | Power | Eng. Type | Speed | Type |
|------|-------|-----------|-------|------|
| 102 | 6.5bhp | 2-cycle | n.a. | mini-trail |
| 100 | 4.0bhp | 4-cycle | n.a. | mini-trail |
| 22 | 2.5bhp | 4-cycle | n.a. | mini-road |

| Name | Power | Eng. Type | Speed | Type |
|------|-------|-----------|-------|------|

**TRAIL HORSE Gen. Appliance Man. Co., 6200 N. 16th Street, Omaha, Nebraska**

| Name | Power | Eng. Type | Speed | Type |
|------|-------|-----------|-------|------|
| GTO 100 | 2.5bhp | 4-cycle | 25mph | mini-trail |
| GTO 200 | 3bhp | 4-cycle | 25mph | mini-trail |
| GTO 300 | 3.5bhp | 4-cycle | 25mph | mini-trail |
| GTO 800 | 3.5bhp | 4-cycle | 20mph | mini-road |
| GTO 850 | 3.5bhp | 4-cycle | 20mph | mini-road |
| GTO 880 | 3.5bhp | 4-cycle | 25mph | mini-road |
| GTO 500 | 5bhp | 4-cycle | 30mph | mini-trail |
| GTO 1500 | 5bhp | 4-cycle | 30mph | mini-enduro |

**VALIANT MAN 4000 Toulouse, New Orleans, Louisiana**

| Name | Power | Eng. Type | Speed | Type |
|------|-------|-----------|-------|------|
| Simplex | 4bhp | 4-cycle | 30mph | mini-enduro |
| Simplex | 5bhp | 4-cycle | 30mph | mini-enduro |

**YAMAHA P.O. Box 54540, Los Angeles, California**

| Name | Power | Eng. Type | Speed | Type |
|------|-------|-----------|-------|------|
| JT-1 | 4.5bhp | 2-cycle | 35mph | mini-enduro |

The following manufacturers had not supplied sufficient information at press time for inclusion in our chart, but all make mini-cycles worth seeing. Check these machines as you would those listed above.

**ALLIED LEISURE Allied Leisure Inc., Box 5411, Lansing, Michigan**

60 models—3-5bhp—10″ 12″ 14″ tires

**ARCO Alexander-Reynolds Corp., 123 S. Newman St., Hackensack, New Jersey**

Eight models from .5-5bhp. Other statistics not available.

**BARRIS KUSTOM Seeker Engineering, 401 E. Alondra Blvd., Gardena, California**

| | | | | |
|------|-------|-----------|-------|------|
| Calif Chopper | 3.5bhp | 4-cycle | | mini-road |

**BONHAM CORP. Bonham Corp., P.O. Box 858, Provo, Utah**

| | | | |
|------|-------|-----------|-------|
| Mini Gote | 7bhp | mini-trail | Other stats. n.a. |

| Name | Power | Eng. Type | Speed | Type |
|---|---|---|---|---|
| **CAT   Muskin, 225 Acacia Street, Colton, California** | | | | |
| 350S | 3.5bhp | 4-cycle | | mini-road |
| 400X | 4bhp | 4-cycle | | mini-trail |
| 400TS | 4bhp | 4-cycle | | mini-road |
| Eliminator | 4bhp | 4-cycle | | mini-road |
| Seven others—statistics n.a. | | | | |
| | | | | |
| **DURA BIKE   K-C Man. Co. Inc., P.O. Box 1167, Quincy, Florida** | | | | |
| Dura Bike | 3bhp | 4-cycle | 20mph | mini-road |
| Dura Bike | 4bhp | 4-cycle | 20mph | mini-road |
| | | | | |
| **HEALD INC.   Dept. MB-8, P.O. Box 1148, Benton Harbor, Michigan** | | | | |
| Two Models—kits only | | | | |
| | | | | |
| **MANCO   3337 Freeman St., Fort Wayne, Indiana** | | | | |
| Little Gen | 3.5bhp | 4-cycle | | mini-trail |
| Little Gen | 5bhp | 4-cycle | | mini-trail |
| | | | | |
| **ROGUE   Mark IV Metal Products, 1705 West 134th St., Gardena, California** | | | | |
| Rogue | 4bhp | 4-cycle | | mini-trail |

## ALL-TERRAIN CYCLES

The All-Terrain Vehicle, or ATV, is a new machine designed to go anywhere. Most commonly it has six or eight oversized tires and recently two- and three-wheeled versions called ATC's, or All-Terrain Cycles, have appeared. Like ATV's they are rough, rugged and great fun. Predictably they are becoming very popular.

They're so new that a typical form has yet to be developed, which means you can see them in all shapes and sizes with varying degrees of power and sophistication.

As in ATV's the tires are the most unusual items. They are big, about 18 inches in diameter and 8 to 10 inches wide, soft, with air pressure of 3 to 7 pounds.

They are designed to improve flotation, that is performance on soft, marginal terrain.

**BONHAM** **Bonham Corp. P.O. Box 858, Provo, Utah**
The Tote Gote is one of the oldest ATC's around, predating the term ATV itself. It's without some of the all-terrain capabilities of the others, but able to pack a great deal of gear or whatever. It comes with a 7 horse, 4-stroke engine which affords it lots of power. The horsepower increase that represents is new, but the rugged reliability of the Tote Gote remains the same.

**DUNE CYCLE** **A.P.E. Products, 13727 Excelsior Dr., Santa Fe Springs, California**
Dune Cycle makes four models, the 100-S, the 100, the Flat Tracker-S, and the Flat Tracker. The differences between them are negligible, the only substantial variation being the space-grip tires on the 100 models and the track-grid tires on the Flat Trackers.

The Dune Cycles are the first of several ATC's with three wheels, which seems a good design for rough-ground beasts. All four models have 5 horsepower engines running through torque converters to produce a top speed of around 30 miles an hour.

**EL BURRO** **Worth Ind. Processing Cp., Lexington, Michigan**
The El Burro is as close to a typical ATC as you can get. The super-side, high-flotation tires each have one square foot of contact with the ground. There is no suspension—the tires fulfill that task too.

The Burro is driven by a 5-horsepower Briggs and Stratton engine with a Comet Torque Converter that boosts the top speed higher than the 20mph claimed for the old models. It has disc brakes and a good travel range with a claimed gas mileage of 120 per gallon.

The Burro is one of the better camping ATC's because it has lots of room for equipment or game and has the power and gearing to pack quite a load.

**GILL MFG.    Gill Mfg., 3507 N. Kenton Ave., Chicago, Illinois**

The Gill people call their ATC the Trail Hawk. It weighs 125 pounds and comes with a 7 horsepower Tecumseh 4-stroke. It's hindered by the use of a two-speed automatic transmission which isn't adequate for the country in which it will be used.

The Trail Hawk uses narrower tires than the other machines in the field, but is still a capable bush bike. Another plus is the (relatively) low price which is many dollars less than the majority of its competitors.


**HONDA    American Honda Motor Co., P.O. Box 50—100 W. Alondra Blvd., Gardena, California**

Honda has come out with a unique three wheeler, powered by their seven horsepower 89cc bike engine. It's one of the heaviest ATC's at a slight 196 pounds, but the immense 22X11 inch tires more than support that and the heaviest rider.

Rather atypical of the rest of the ATC field is the fact that the Honda can carry only one rider, and has no provisions for carrying gear. Made just for people who enjoy riding, the Honda can be quickly broken down and put into a small space for easy transportation and storage.

The transmission is an automatic four speed, which has enough range to pull slowly or to cruise at a rapid rate.


**LARKIN IND    Larkin Aircraft Co., Watsonville, California**

Probably the most revolutionary of the bunch is the mini-ATC from Larkin. Instead of a rear wheel, the Hill Cat has a pivoting two-wheel structure in back with both wheels driving. It can climb almost anything and has twice the traction of most other bikes.

It is limited by the fact that it uses standard mini-bike wheels. An exciting engineering feat with the potential of this one deserves more attention in the area of tires and engine, too, since the one they use has only 4 horses.

A little too much like a mini-bike to call itself an ATC, the Hill Cat isn't enough like an ATC to accurately call itself one of those either. Even with its limitations, the Hill Cat is a worthy machine.

## MOBILITY UNLIMITED  Magna American Corp. Raymond, Miss.

Called the Amphikitty, Mobility Unlimited's ATC is reminiscent of the original boony bikes. Its giant tires hold enough air at low pressure to make it float, and its carrying capacity marks it as a good pack machine. The 5 horsepower engine is a Briggs and Stratton 4-stroke that sends the kitty over obstacles at up to 20 miles per hour. In addition to having many of the luxury items—fiberglass fenders, chain guard, and big, two-person seat that set it up for packing—the Amphikitty is one of only two ATC's with lights.

The design is basic and makes the bike easy to maintain. The frame is a simple double downtube cradle affair that is big enough to dwarf the engine and is long enough for lots of gear or another passenger. Carrying both isn't recommended with the low power engine, the Achilles heel of an otherwise very good machine.

## PACESETTER  Pacesetter Ent. Inc., Cascade, Iowa

Pacesetter makes the Trail Ram, a bike that qualifies as the Cadillac of the ATC scene. It weighs in at 150 pounds, but has a 7 horsepower Tecumseh to push it as fast and with as much power as anyone could want. A Comet torque converter and #40 chain connect the engine to the wheels and do their job well in between.

The Pacesetter is the other ATC with lights, for duty after dark in an emergency or just for fun. Its tank is one of the largest at 1.5 gallons, but for long trips, it should be replaced with a larger one.

The Pacesetter has two features that set it above the rest of the ATC's. The first is the seat. Unfortunately, most manufacturers seem to think that if you can take the rigors of cycling, you can accept a saddle-sore rear too. But Pacesetter has provided a well-sprung, amply padded, comfortable seat that will take the misery out of sitting down after a day of riding.

The second feature is the most important. The Pacesetter has leading link front suspension, something it shares with some of the world's best motorcycles, and something that puts its handling in another dimension.

**RANKIN MFG   Rankin Mfg. Inc., 924 N. Saginaw St., Durand, Michigan**

Rankin makes a machine they call the Terre Cat. They put a 5 horse Clinton 4-stroke in it and run the power to the rear wheel through a torque converter. The tires are 18-inch diameter, 9-inch wide spade grip jobs covered by full coverage fenders.

Put together it's a good combination, made by one of the few companies that also has the intelligence to include a spark arrestor.

**TRAIL BREAKER   Rokon Inc., Keene, New Hampshire**

Built for off-road use, the Rokon *Trail Breaker* features hollow-spun aluminum wheels and weighs only 108 pounds. Already proven by the U.S. Forest Service, the cycle's unique engineering allows it to ford streams to two feet deep and to climb grades up to 60 degrees. The ignition is waterproof and power is supplied by an 8hp two-cycle. Kick and rope-pull starting systems are available. The rig has two-wheel drive, each wheel independently powered with a special coupling that lets each wheel find its own rotation speed when climbing over obstacles.

**TREDWELL   Tredwell Mfg., Box 610, Prince George, British Columbia**

The Partner is Tredwell's ATC. The Partner starts out as a regular ATC, with a 5 horse Briggs and Stratton and a one-speed transmission with clutch. The two tires are both 11X20 low pressure (2 to 4 psi) for more traction.

More money will buy a list of attachments as long as your arm. Like two speeds. Or a gun carrying case and auxiliary gas tank. Or both. Of course there are skis that mount on the front for snow or, if you want, you can get a Partner with 2-wheel drive.

Instead of buying another for a friend, you can just buy another rear wheel that attaches to the first rear wheel to give three drive wheels. Don't buy an ATC without seeing a Partner.

### TRI CART Sperry-Rand Corp., New Holland Group, New Holland, Pennsylvania

The Tri Cart is another three wheeler. It looks like the Dune Cycle in that you ride it more like a small car than like a bike. But the Tri Cart has 11 horses and a 230cc 4-stroke engine that spirits it along at a quick 45 miles per hour. Like the futuristic beast it is, its controls are consolidated in the handle-bars. Lift them up to go faster, push them to go slowly, and in either case, pay a great deal to own it.

Chapter 5

# *LEARNING TO RIDE*

ALTHOUGH MOTORCYCLE RIDING is easy, the first stages can be difficult. A new rider can't learn on public streets because there are no "learner's" permits and he can't be licensed until he can prove he knows how to handle a bike. It is a perplexing situation.

In most cities there are no off-street training areas, few courses and fewer teachers. But the picture is changing. As motorcycles become popular, high schools, dealers, and private riders are taking a new look at the problem. One such person is Mrs. Bill Lohrke of Eugene, Oregon. Mrs. Lohrke (pronounced *Lurkee*) has a plan to teach new bike owners cycle basics quickly, easily and legally.

She and her husband, a mechanic for Lane County, Oregon, have been riding for 14 years, logging more than 140,000 accident-free miles. Last year they held a course in cycle safety at the Lane Community College near Eugene and plan to repeat the instruction this year. The course will cost five dollars per student with bikes furnished to those without them by cycle dealers from the Eugene-Springfield area.

The instruction is a beginning, but Mrs. Lohrke feels there should be more. She insists state motor vehicle departments should provide:

    1. Special cycle education courses

2. A rider's manual and examination specifically for cycle owners.
3. A continuing public relations effort designed to bring a better understanding between automobile and cycle owners.

Riders in several cities are pressing for similar courses and training has been proposed as an adjunct to Driver's Education in some high schools. But aside from Eugene, chances are that the only instruction currently available is from a cycle dealer. One manufacturer, Yamaha, has produced a complete basic training course so thorough you can learn all of the tricks of street and dirt riding easily. The course is designed to function at a dealer level, but the text is so well planned it could be used in schools with few changes.

If you are learning to ride we know of no better instruction. With the kind permission of the Yamaha International Corporation, Montebello, California, the following material is condensed from their excellent book, *Common Sense Tips for Safe Sportcycling* by Jim Jingu and Don Gately.

The riding habits you form while learning will stick with you the rest of your riding years. Bad habits are difficult to break; therefore it is important to take the time to learn to ride properly.

Learn to operate the controls before you start the machine. The clutch is operated by the lever on the left handlebar. The accelerator is controlled with the right handgrip. The rear brake is operated with one foot, usually on the right. The opposite foot controls the gear shift. The lever on the right handlebar operates the front wheel brake.

Place the cycle on its center stand. Practice operating the controls while the bike is on the stand. Concentrate on what you would do in stopping and starting. Make the motions instinctive.

Then start the engine. Starting procedures vary from model to model, but there are general rules to remember: Make certain the transmission is in neutral before you begin. Most cycles have a neutral indicator on the speedometer panel which lights when the ignition switch is turned on and the bike is in neutral. But be sure to remember—these indicators are not completely reliable. Make certain the gas petcock is turned on. The correct position is usually straight up and down. The petcock is usually on the bottom of the fuel tank at the rear left side. Turn on the key and, if the engine is cold, put on the choke. The choke is found on the left handlebar or on the carburetor.

Depress the kick starter as you turn the gas about half way. Don't be afraid to kick hard. The common fault most beginners make is not following through in the kick. Use body weight to turn the engine over. Repeated kicking may be necessary but it is possible that the engine may become flooded. If you smell gas, let off on the choke and continue the kicking process, but alternate the throttle from full to half positions. In extreme cases it may be necessary to remove the spark plug and clean away excess gas. After the engine starts, let it warm a few minutes, gradually turning the choke off.

Take your first rides in low gear. After the engine is warmed, pull in the clutch lever and kick the bike into first gear. Let the clutch out slowly while turning the gas on one-quarter to one-half throttle. You may have to try this combination several times before you can achieve a smooth start. Now practice riding in a straight line, starting, stopping and starting until you can do everything smoothly. Pretend you see a red light and must stop quickly.

Beware of the front brake. It has more braking action

than the rear one. Do not apply it when the bike is not running in a straight line. Do not "slam" it on tightly, but apply the brake gradually. Use it in unison with the rear brake. Eventually you will come to rely on the front brake more than the rear, but do not be in a hurry to master this technique. Avoid using the front brake when the wheel is turned or when you are on anything other than ideal riding surfaces.

Ride in circles. Once you are used to the process of stopping and starting and combining the gas, clutch and brakes, try riding in circles. Start with large, easy circles and gradually diminish the size. This will help you develop the feel of balance and turning. You will notice that turning is accomplished more by leaning than from actually turning the handlebars. Use knee pressure against the fuel tank as you turn.

Now, ride straight and shift. Gear shift patterns vary from motorcycle to motorcycle and even from model to model within a given brand. Be sure you are "checked out" by the dealer on the way your machine shifts before you start. Begin with low and shift upward to "high"; then go back down through the gears for braking action. Once you have completed this process several times you are ready for a longer run. If you have a license, try the street. Try a few figure eight's and S's just to be sure.

Before you venture into traffic, get plenty of practice riding on quiet streets. Parking lots are great, if they are big. Don't ride with a passenger until you have plenty of experience riding solo.

A word of caution: Riding a motorcycle on an unpaved road is not the same as riding on a paved surface. Even some veteran motorcyclists are not at home in the dirt the first time they try it. You should learn to ride on a paved road. If you go into the woods, take it easy and slow. Practice in the dirt before you start on a trail ride.

## The Art of Perpetual Defensive Driving

It has been established statistically that more motorcycle accidents are the fault of automobile drivers than the fault of the motorcyclists themselves. For this reason it is essential to practice the art of "defensive riding."

Many youngsters learning to ride cycles have never driven automobiles and most do not receive instructions on operating cycles in any class, school or clinic. They are merely taught by a more experienced motorcyclist. They therefore do not have the advantage of having had previous experience in traffic conditions or in the operation of a motor vehicle.

Never forget that all the rules and courtesies of the road apply to sportcycles to an even greater extent than they do to automobiles. Why? Because the rider of a two-wheel machine rarely wins an encounter with the driver of an automobile or truck. Safety for your sake dictates that you obey all traffic rules and courtesies at all times.

You cannot expect to take minor liberties with safe driving rules to save a little time. Whenever you stretch the law, you are in the wrong and expose yourself to possible serious injury.

## Know All Traffic Regulations

The same traffic rules and regulations apply to cycles that apply to automobiles, but there is a tendency on the part of some cyclists to disregard rules because of the maneuverability and ease of handling their vehicles in traffic. The first step towards operating your sportcycle safely is knowing and obeying all traffic laws.

## Hand Signals

Hand signals are known throughout the United States. The left arm extended straight out always indicates a left turn. It is more difficult to signal while riding a sportcycle than while driving a car. Since you will probably need both hands and both feet to control your machine in a turning, passing or stopping maneuver, you should allow enough time to safely remove your left hand from the controls to give the proper signal. Of course, in an emergency situation demanding immediate reaction, signaling is almost impossible. Mechanical turn signals, as a rule on smaller machines, are not large enough, bright enough, or far enough apart to be noticed by other motorists, especially in bright daylight, and you should not depend on them.

## Road Surface

The condition of the road you are riding on is much more critical than in an automobile. Rocks, sand, leaves, ice and chuckholes can all cause you to lose control. Loose stone from side roads is often present at country intersections, and this may cause a momentary (and deadly) loss of traction. Patches, cracks, holes, ruts and sharp edges are much more frequent on country roads and highways than on superhighways. On hot days, tar liquefies, and before you know it, your tire tread is covered and filled with tar. On humid days, moisture may condense on the road surface and make it slippery. One danger you should always look for is the remains of a highway accident: glass, oil, water, plastic, or metal parts scattered or spilled on the pavement. Any one could cause you to have an accident.

## Dogs, Pedestrians, Children

Always be especially alert in residential areas because children often dash into the road from between parked cars or other obstacles to your vision. Dogs are particularly prone to chasing motorcycles—the noise seems to attract them.

## Noise

Unnecessarily loud motorcycles go a long way toward giving the public an unfavorable image of motorcycles. But there is a more important reason for keeping your cycle legally muffled and as quiet as possible: a loud motorcycle can be dangerously distracting. A motorcyclist in heavy traffic or passing cars may startle a motorist so badly with an excessively loud motorcycle that the driver of the car may unintentionally swerve into the rider.

## Streetcar Tracks or Railroad Crossings

Railroad or streetcar crossings require extreme caution. Many crossings are in a poor state of repair. Some are raised above the surface of the road, others are below the surface. Some cross the highway at an angle. Slow down, signal the cars behind you and cross the tracks carefully at as straight an angle as possible. If the road is wet, crossings can be even more dangerous.

## Passengers

When you ride with a passenger, be certain he knows the correct riding procedure. The passenger must always sit on the seat with one leg on each side. Never permit a female passenger to ride sidesaddle; she will always feel off-balance. The passenger should hold on to you lightly with hands resting on your waist, prepared to hold more tightly as necessary, or to the seat strap on two-passenger buddy seats. The position keeps the center of gravity of the passenger close to you for a much better job of control. Tell your passenger not to assume the responsibility of balancing you or your machine, especially in a turn. Instruct your passenger to keep his feet on the foot rests at all times, especially when you stop. Passengers, no matter how young, should always ride behind you. If the child is too young to safely ride behind you, it is too young to ride. Always be certain your passenger wears a fastened helmet.

## Carrying Luggage

When you take luggage or a pack, make sure it is fastened securely. Everything should be behind you so nothing can interfere with the control of your machine. Nothing is more annoying (and potentially dangerous) than having part or all of your load come loose. Luggage racks suitable for the appearance and construction of your machine should be available from your dealer.

## Travel at Normal Traffic Speed

In most states the law requires that you travel at the normal flow of traffic. If the speed limit is 50mph, for example, but traffic is heavy enough to be moving only at 35mph, you would be violating the law to try to travel faster than that. It is dangerous to assume that because your vehicle is maneuverable and has rapid acceleration that you can try to "get to the front" or "snake" your way through traffic. Stay in line.

## Don't Get Caught in a Sandwich

Always keep plenty of room between yourself, the car in front and behind. The trick is to regulate the distance between yourself and the car following you. If you crowd the car ahead and the car behind tailgates, you are in the explosive situation known as the "sandwich." This is much more dangerous at highway speed than at city speed. If the car driver behind you persists in tailgating, signal him to pass as soon as it is safe. Slow down as he passes you to help him get around you faster.

## Do Not Follow too Closely

Following too closely in a car is always a serious thing to do, but on a motorcycle it is downright fool-hardy. Most motorcycles have braking superior to a car's. As a result, many riders get into the habit of following too closely. This can be dangerous, not only because inattention can have you run into the car ahead of you, but also because ultra-quick stopping can get you rammed in the rear by a car behind you who could not stop as quickly. If you follow too closely your vision of the road ahead is greatly reduced.

## Overtaking Another Vehicle

One of the most common causes of accidents is improper passing. Never pass unless you can see the on-coming traffic for a more than ample distance and are absolutely certain you have time to pass the vehicle in front of you, regardless of how fast the on-coming traffic may be moving. Be alert for vehicles coming from side roads. Pass the vehicle smoothly and steadily, giving him a wide berth.

Whenever you are going to overtake another vehicle look over your shoulder first. Do not depend solely on your rearview mirrors. Develop the habit of looking in your mirrors frequently even when you are not preparing to pass. The more you know about the total traffic situation—front and rear—the safer you will be.

## Night Driving

Driving at night requires more attention and caution than in the daylight. Check your lighting frequently to be sure you have as much visibility as possible. Always wear clear goggles and should they become scratched or stained, do not use them at night. Headlight glare reflected on such marks on goggles or glasses can blind you. When approaching oncoming traffic or following closely behind another vehicle, always ride with your low beam light on. Watch the shoulder of the road and the white line when oncoming lights reduce your visibility. Always slow down at night.

## Wind

Heavy winds can cause unusual riding conditions. If the wind is at your back, you will find that your engine requires less gas to maintain a given speed. This is called a tailwind. In this instance, check your speedometer occasionally to make sure you are not speeding. If you are riding into a wind, you will find your power is reduced. Under extreme conditions, it may be necessary to lower your head and chest down over the gas tank. This is rather hazardous because you lose some of your balance and visibility. It is therefore recommended only if you cannot proceed at a safe enough speed not to hamper other traffic. Winds coming at you from a side direction or at an angle can be distracting at best, and dangerous at worst. You will find you will have to lean slightly in the direction from which the wind is coming to compensate for the force of the wind, particularly if it is a heavy wind. Also, trucks, busses, trailers or even cars approaching you from the opposite direction or overtaking you even on a calm day can produce a draft which could be hazardous if you are not braced for it. If you see a situation like this arising, simply tighten your grip on the controls, crouch a bit lower on the machine and be prepared for a hard force of wind.

Riding in heavy wind can be more fatiguing because you must brace for sudden jolts or drafts. Always consider wind factors if you plan long rides.

### Riding in Unfamiliar Areas

Traffic laws and road conditions vary from state to state and locality to locality. It is always wise to check with the highway patrol or other authorities to learn the laws and conditions under which you will be driving before venturing into areas with which you are unfamiliar.

Never smoke while riding a motorcycle. Not only can blowing sparks start disastrous fires, but ashes can blow in your eyes and impair your vision. Wise cyclists park their machines and walk away from them when they wish to smoke. If they are in a wooded area they only smoke at places designated for smoking.

When riding in groups, do not ride directly side by side. The rider to the right should be slightly to the rear of the rider to the left.

Chapter 6

# *HOW TO FORM A CLUB*

EVERY CITY should have at least one motorcycle club and, if there is none in your town (or if there is a need for another), form a club now. It's easier than you think. A club can do a lot to establish good community relations and will help solve mutual problems. It can provide interesting activities to bring riders together on an equal footing and, perhaps the most basic reason of all, will provide a place where riders can meet as friends.

Where to meet? In the beginning consider a dealer's store. It is the logical place for a first meeting, if not for after that. If no other suitable arrangements can be made, contact a city official to see if you can use a schoolroom, a public hall or even an empty store. As a last resort try a member's home.

To start you need a list of prospective members. You can begin with a list of friends, but a good club needs wider scope than that. Let dealers help. They can supply the names and addresses of riders who might make good members. Send each person a letter or post card inviting them to the initial meeting. Be sure to set the time and place. Then follow up a few days before the meeting with a reminder.

The purpose of the first meeting is to show guests that a club, with the activities it can offer, is a good thing. Plan your first program to illustrate these points. Prove to everyone that a club can be good for *all* members. In the beginning forget about formalities. Move around the room as the invited guests come in and talk to everyone. Break the barriers: be sure everyone meets everyone else.

Then begin the business meeting. Make your point and select a temporary chairman. Let him appoint an acting secretary. Remember that the future conduct of members is determined to a large measure by the manner in which the first meeting is conducted. Be brief, concise and to the point. Follow a sensible plan. If you have doubts about the way a meeting should be run, get a copy of *Robert's Rules of Order* at your library.*

If most of the guests are in favor of a club begin by adopting a constitution. It determines the success of the club, future meetings and members. It eliminates most of the openings for argument and starts club activities on the proper footing. A suggested constitution is included at the end of this chapter. As you progress with the reading of the constitution be sure every member understands each point. Settle questions of initiation fees and dues promptly. Don't make the fees too high and above all keep expenses down.

Proceed with the selection of officers. These are elected from the guests in this order: president, vice-president, secretary, treasurer, road captain and referee. Vote for officials one at a time. Get as many nominees as you can, distribute ballots—one to each guest—then vote. Collect the votes and count them. The man with the highest count is elected.

The president should then appoint a membership committee and they should draft a membership blank. Then have all people present join the club, paying their dues to the secretary. You now have a club. The secretary should make a record of all dues, issuing a

* *Also available in paperback from Pyramid Books.*

receipt or membership card to each member. If there is time at the first meeting appoint the various committees to carry on the club work—entertainment, house and tour committees are basic. If there is no time at the first meeting, make the selection of committee the first order of business at the second meeting. With the committees in operation a club is ready to function.

The officers should be prepared to give their best and in turn should be guaranteed the support of the full membership. Since the officers have been selected by a majority vote, they should have the support of every member, even those who did not vote for them. If your officers prove unsatisfactory after a year's trial, elect others. But in the beginning give them every chance for success. If you are elected or appointed to a committee, do the very best you can. Support your club and its officers by avoiding friction. Talk motorcycling *in general,* not by *makes* of cycles. Keep partisan ideas out of your club.

## Club Affiliation

To gain the most enjoyment from a club membership consider affiliating with a national cycle association. The American Motorcycle Association is the most popular, although there are others. Membership in the A.M.A. will offer many benefits. For example, the Association has done much to win the public's respect. They have fought for and succeeded in obtaining reductions of licensing fees in several states and have worked hard to combat unjust legislation wherever it appears.

Among its major achievements is an annual Safety Campaign in which all affiliated clubs and riders take part. The success of this campaign has done much to increase the popularity of riding. Furthermore, events sponsored by the individual member clubs receive gen-

erous publicity locally because of the prestige of the
A.M.A. affiliation.

In addition the A.M.A. provides a thorough set of
rules and regulations covering every phase of motorcycle activity. These uniform rules give all members a
basis by which their abilities can be judged fairly. The
popularity of such uniformity can be seen from the
large number of rallys, hill climbs, field meets and other
events sponsored under A.M.A. sanction each year.
And the orderly manner in which the events are carried
out makes a distinct hit with spectators. They invariably
leave feeling a little better about motorcycling.

Today, through the combined efforts of the A.M.A.
and its member clubs, the sport is growing in size and
popularity. Your club will receive many times the value
of its charter in factors which can be measured in more
than dollars and cents. One of the major benefits is the
opportunity to participate in the annual Activity Contest. It is offered to help club members maintain
enthusiastic interest throughout the year. An attractive
trophy is donated to each participating club with ten or
more members. Two trophies are given to clubs with
memberships of 22 or more.

Another valuable Association benefit is an opportunity to win the attractive Safety Award. These are
given at the close of each Safety Campaign to affiliated
clubs which, through proper safe riding practices, have
achieved a creditable record on the basis of monthly
reports.

To affiliate with the A.M.A., it is necessary that
there be at least ten club members in good standing
with the A.M.A. when your application is submitted.

### Hints for Officers

No officer can hope to remember all of the rules
governing a meeting, but you can go a long way toward

## SOME OF THE LATEST MODELS

You can credit Honda with the idea and the bike that started the small cycle and trail bike boom. Paradoxically, their relatively new 750 is big and one of the best touring cycles on the market.

New from Bronco, the Apache 100, a lightweight trail machine introduced at Daytona. Engine has an extremely flat power band and isn't "peaky." Four-speed transmission, 12 hp at as much as 8,000 rpm.

Suzuki makes a bike for every purpose — a long line of good cycles. Here, the Suzuki 250, a good general purpose machine.

BMW 750 — an excellent touring cycle. The record includes a New York to Los Angeles speed record and an Alaska to Tierra del Fuego run.

Sachs begins with a basic engine and adds power as needed. This version is the Enduro. Like other models, it features an Earles-type front fork.

Puch features lightweight machines ideal for competition. Bike has Girling rear suspension, Magura controls, Ceriani front forks, and Bosch electrical equipment among a number of custom touches.

Cimatti offers 10 models this year. Frame is double-cradle type and bike has many desirable features. Cross Competizione versions are especially impressive— the 175, for example, can carry even a large rider at high speeds.

Bridgestone builds several bikes reminiscent of the older scramblers. Every one is street ready. Dollar for dollar these are excellent buys for riders who want good street machines.

Kawasaki calls the all new 250E Enduro their secret weapon for 1971. For highway travel, a top speed of 85 mph. For cross-country, 9 full inches of ground clearance, 55-inch wheelbase, upswept and tucked-in pipes, and a completely closed magneto.

Harley-Davidson's big-inch V-twin holds more records at Bonneville and the nation's drag strips than any other engine. The 1971 Sportsters offer blistering torque from a new 900cc engine.

Moto Guzzi, an excellent touring machine. This year the firm offers only its 750cc Ambassador. In place of chain, the cycle has a distinctive direct drive.

The Dunstall Norton 750 Export. It features disc brakes built into the front forks, an engine that puts out 66bhp and a top speed of 131 mph.

Up front, Yamaha's TR2-B 250—it holds longest winning streak in AMA racing history, taking Daytona 6 years straight.

Yamaha's TR2-B 350 road racer. It has led the best of the 750's.

## USEFUL ACCESSORIES

Two people ride comfortably on new 25" buddy seat designed for Stellar mini-bike models. Kit includes seat, folding footrests, all hardware. Available from Stellar Electronics & Mfg. Co., Plainview, N.Y.

These Moto-Cross racing pants are made from soft, durable high-quality leather and feature rubber pads in hips and knees, zippered legs and pockets, and a mesh rayon-type lining. From Webco.

Famous Preston Petty unbreakable plastic fenders are now available in 6 colors. Practically indestructible, they carry a one-year unconditional guarantee. From Webco.

These tighter, stronger, more durable fork boots are made from amazing E.P.R., and defy weather, ozone and wear. Feature a 3-ridge inside-seal "wiper" to assure dust-free operation. From Webco.

A lightweight, strong center stand for almost any cycle. Fully adjustable. From Webco.

For increased stability under unusually rough riding conditions, this front fork suspension kit offers progressive wound full-length fork springs, precision-machined matched dampening units and heavy-duty wipers.

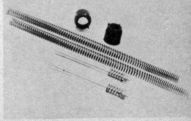

# THE WORLD OF MINI-BIKES

A three-time AMA Grand National Champion on a mini-bike — Bart Markel, 1970 winner, on a Bonanza Ace 100.

Trail riding a mini! At Saddleback Park in Southern California, a Bonanza mini-cross cleared all trails in a half-mile scrambles track.

Gary Nixon, GNC two years in a row, tries out a mini-bike. It has added trail and rake to create a stable ride. In stock form, the machine sells for just a little over $300.

Who says you can't race mini-bikes? The leap, startling as it seems, is safer than it looks.

New Bonanza Mid-Cycle, smaller than a standard, handles superbly and is a great machine for youngsters to learn on.

A mini-bike is a handy thing at a cycle race. Here a Honda is lowered to the pavement for use in running short errands.

Dune cycle converted to skis. Front wheel is replaced with a ski and the low pressure, high flotation rear tires stay high in the snow. Produced by A.P.E. Products, California.

The go-anywhere, do-anything Maxi Super sports a 5 hp (with alternator) Tecumseh engine, adjustable internal expanding brakes, full front and rear suspension, heavy-duty #420 chain, and a bucket of exciting extras.

The Dune Cycle, A.P.E. Products, is available in four models and can be used on a variety of marginal terrains. Five-horsepower engine is standard.

Two-wheel drive is the secret of Rokon's success. Each wheel has independent power and a special coupling allows each one to find its own speed. Hollow rims give bouyance and reduced weight, and low-pressure tires have excellent flotation with good bite.

Honda's 3-wheel all-terrain cycle features a husky 7 hp 89cc engine. It has 4-speed automatic transmission, and the heft and power to deliver plenty of go in rough terrain. The machine can be disassembled to fit in the trunk of a standard car.

Honda offers two mini trail machines and one Road 50 model. (This, the Mini Trail 70 CT-70.) The horsepower ranges from 1.85 to 5, offering a choice of cycles for almost every use.

The Hawk from Power-Dyne features a 172cc American Lauson engine with 10-inch wheels and an upswept exhaust just like larger trail machines. Excellent for a variety of off-highway riding.

Bonanza takes on the big bikes with this Mid-Cycle— a new concept in small bikes. Larger than a mini, it has 16-inch wheels, 100cc engine and has set two world records at Bonneville.

## TECHNICAL TOUCHES

Trail and street sprockets vary in the number of teeth, and a change is required for optimum performance in each environment. Some bikes offer an easy automatic changeover; others require more mechanical changes.

Correct tires are an important part of all riding, but in racing (as shown here) they are essential. These are for dirt-track competition, similar to those for track-street use. Pure trail machines work better with knobby tires.

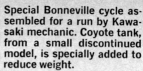

Special Bonneville cycle assembled for a run by Kawasaki mechanic. Coyote tank, from a small discontinued model, is specially added to reduce weight.

Socket wrenches are versatile, handy tools. Shown here, left to right, top to bottom: long handle, standard handle, ratchet, extensions, universal, several socket heads, and at bottom a torque wrench.

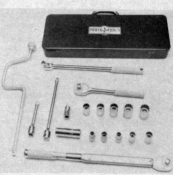

Spark plug wrench is a must. Most bike tool kits offer some type of socket or plug device, but consider adding a special plug-type socket. It speeds up work.

Transmission is important, especially on trail machines. Four and five speeds are most common. Exhaust protection plate is another sign of quality. (Bike is Harley-Davidson Rapido.)

For carrying passengers, choose a wide, long seat like this—room and comfort for two. For trails use a single seat: it allows room behind for a carrying rack, important when camping, touring or carrying out game.

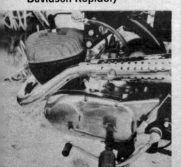

Competition, trails and specially tuned machines usually feature tuned expansion chambers, which reduce back pressure, improve power and performance and add a custom-racing look.

You should be able to see the instrument panel *and* the road without difficulty. 1971 Electra Glide, from Harley, has a new easy-to-see tank-mounted cluster. Dials are large, illuminated, designed for fast reading.

### How to Read Spark Plugs

*Left, Normal wear.* If plugs have light tan or gray deposits and a small amount of electrode wear (not more than .005 inch gap growth), plugs can probably be recleaned, regapped and reinstalled.

*Center, Carbon fouled.* Plug with carbon deposits indicates need for a replacement plug one heat range warmer. If carbon deposits are forming on plug recommended for particular engine, a too-rich fuel mixture is indicated.

*Right, Overheated.* Plugs will have dead white insulator and badly eroded electrodes. The next colder heat range is recommended and it is advisable that ignition timing is not over advanced.

Don't carry passengers until you have experience riding alone. Passengers should grasp you around the waist or hold the hand support on the seat. They should not try to control the cycle—leaning on turns—but should ride "with the machine."

Sit squarely in the saddle, arms comfortably extended, body balanced over the center of the cycle. Riding habits formed while learning stay with you; make the very first rides right and safe. (Bike is Bonanza.)

Brake and throttle controls are mounted on the right. Front brake controls only on full-sized cycles.

Clutch control is on the left. A good rear vision mirror is an essential safety item for street cycles—be sure you have one.

Dick Mann, number four rider this season, entered the Sacramento one-mile event with a partially healed broken leg. He took off the cast against doctor's orders and rode until the pain stopped him. Here, testing his machine, a BSA.

The Grand National Champion, Gene Romero, is shown taking a corner at the Sacramento race. That form is part of the reason Romero is a top winner.

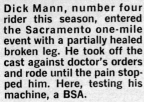

Enduro racing is very popular in many parts of the country and often includes such things as the water hazard shown here in a Southern California race.

Gary Nixon leading through a corner at Sacramento. Gene Romero won; it was the event that lifted him into number one rankings, guaranteeing the Grand National Championship.

An amazing sight at Bonneville! Record runs with a mini-bike. Records won included: PSA-AG-174 class at 92.5 mph and an A-AG-100 run at 79.77 mph—fast for a mini no matter how you look at it. Designer and builder of the record bikes was Jack Costella of Bonanza.

For competition fun without the rigors of high-speed riding, try Trials. They're a test of ability over varied rough terrain rather than a test of speed.

A special piece of equipment is worn by dirt track riders—a "hot shoe" or steel plate made to slide along the ground as riders take the turns. Worn over the left shoe, it's used as support on high-speed turns. Ken Maely is the best-known manufacturer in the circuit and builds the shoes to order at the races—here, at Sacramento.

## TOP-RANKED RIDERS

**Gary Nixon**

**Mert Lawill**

**Gene Romero**

**Eddie Mulder**

**Yvon Duhamel**

**Don Castro**

**Mark Brelsford**

**Bart Markel**

**Charles Palmgren**

**Dick Mann**

**Jim Rice**

Printed in U.S.A.

# YAMAHA '71

# It's a better machine

# Better in the rough.

Yamaha Enduros and Motocross machines are built to withstand all the hard knocks Mother Nature can send your way. With heftier front forks, 5-step adjustable rear suspension, and super-strengthened double-cradle framework. Look over our new crop. Pick out the one that's right for you.

**CT1-C 175cc Enduro**  Big bike torque with the handling of its little brothers. Autolube, wide-ratio 5-speed gearbox, five-port power — the works.

**DT1-E 250cc Enduro**  Enduro front forks let you go over, not around, the rough stuff. With Autolube, wide-ratio 5-speed gearbox. A real winner on and off the road.

**RT1-B 360cc Enduro**
Our big boy that likes to play in the dirt. It's got five-port power, Enduro front forks, 5-speed gearbox and Autolube, too.

**AT1-C 125cc Enduro**
Enduro through and through. With the convenience of electric starting.

**HT1-B 90cc Enduro** Call it a camper's companion or a teenager's best friend — with wide-ratio 5-speed gearbox, Autolube, and exclusive five-port power.

# Motocross dynamite on two wheels.

### AT1-MX 125cc
With close-ratio, 5-speed gearbox. GYT Kit, tuned exhaust and Autolube. A fierce competitor.

### DT1-MX 250cc
Take the checkered flag — with a close-ratio 5-speed gearbox, GYT Kit, tuned exhaust and Autolube.

### RT1-MX 360cc
Don't even bother to look back. It's got a close-ratio 5-speed gearbox, GYT Kit, tuned exhaust, Autolube, and a handling package that just won't quit.

# Mini-Enduro
# Call it, "Son of Enduro."

Less than 36 inches high, yet built like the big Enduros. A 60cc engine. Four-speed constant-mesh gearbox. Autolube oil injection. Improved Enduro front forks. Big waterproof/dustproof safety brakes. And, federal forestry approved spark arrester. Tell yourself it's for the kid.

# Better on the open road.

Yamaha street machines set a whole new pace on the open highway. Our 650 4-stroke twin won last year's Nazareth National hands down. Our 350 R-5B was rated "first overall" by Cycle Magazine in their December '70 "Six Bike 350 Comparison Test." Typical of every street bike we build, they're better machines.

### G6S-B 80cc Street
Get up and go — with a powerful 2-stroke Rotary-valve engine, 4-speed gearbox and Autolube oil injection.

### XS1-B 650cc Street
Our biggest better machine. A four-stroke twin that'll make the other big boys wonder what went by. The only production 650 with a single overhead cam design.

### HS1-B 90cc Street
The little wonder. With five-port power, 5-speed synchro gearbox, Autolube. Riding it is believing it.

### CS3-B 200cc Street
Five-speed gearbox, Autolube, five-port power and heavy-weight stability. Electric starting and excellent brakes.

### R5-B 350cc Street
Beauty and brawn. A two-stroke twin with five-port power, Autolube, Enduro-type front forks and a 5-speed gearbox. Performance with a capital "P."

# YAMAHA '71

Enduro,® Motocross or Street. If it's a Yamaha,

## It's a better machine

## Different strokes
## for
## different folks.

## YAMAHA INTERNATIONAL CORPORATION

P.O. Box 54540, Los Angeles, Calif. 90054 • In Canada: Fred Deeley, Ltd., Vancouver, B.C.

a smooth, easy meeting when you take time to read one manual on ways to conduct meetings. Rules of parliamentary procedure were not developed by one group of men. Instead they evolved over a span of time from the experience of thousands of self-governing organizations. The idea has always been to create a smoothly running organization, free of friction with justice for all.

The principles of running a meeting can be outlined in these few paragraphs:

1. *Get down to business*. Meetings are held to get things done. Make them "business first." Welcome an easy, free presentation of all problems. Aim for open discussion, but control the situation. Let opposing sides have equal time, but be sure a discussion does not take up an entire meeting. Do not turn a meeting into a debate. The objective is to reach a fair and workable solution as quickly as possible.

2. *Remember that the majority rules*. Unanimous agreement is seldom possible—or desirable—and complete agreement is rare. Act on even the most important issues when 51 percent of the membership is in agreement. To be certain take votes with either a show of hands, a voice vote or with a count.

3. *Protect the minority*. The majority rules but it doesn't dominate. Forget dictatorships. If there is a minority opinion you can incorporate into some action, do it. In the meantime respect the rights of the minority. That means this: the right of free speech, the right of secret ballot, a protection by the constitution, bylaws and rules of order and a right to nominate men for office.

4. *Respect human feelings*. A club is made up of individuals and individuals have personal feelings. Respect them. Courtesy must temper all relationships,

business and personal. Keep that foremost at all meetings.

## Suggested constitution for A.M.A. affiliated clubs

*Article No. 1*

This club shall be known as the _____.

*Article No. 2*

Active members shall be male riders of motorcycles, men actively engaged with the trade or motorcycle enthusiasts. Honorary members shall be women motorcycle riders, member's wives, motorcycle enthusiasts and such other persons as the club might decide by a two-thirds vote of those present at any regular meeting so to honor. Only active members shall be entitled to a vote in club affairs or to win any prizes in club activities.

*Article No. 3*

The officers of the club shall be a President, Vice-President, Secretary, Treasurer, Road Captain, and referee and these officers shall constitute the Executive Board.

*Article No. 4*

The duties of President shall be:

To preside at all meetings of the club.

To have general supervision of the affairs of the club.

To appoint any person or committees not otherwise ordered by the club.

To personally represent the club on proper occasions and in business contracts.

To assist all other officers of the club in their records, correspondence and other duties.

To promote interest on the part of each member in club life and activities.

To vote only when one vote is necessary to break a tie.

*Article No. 5*

The duties of the Vice-President shall be:

To perform the duties of the President in his absence.

*Article No. 6*

The duties of the Secretary shall be:

To keep a record of the meetings of the club in the minute book provided for that purpose.

To send out notices of regular and special meetings.

To handle all club correspondence.

To perform such other duties as generally fall to that office.

*Article No. 7*

The duties of Treasurer shall be:

To collect dues from all members.

To collect all other money due the club.

To make all payments from the club funds when so ordered by the club.

To keep an account of all money matters.

To make a statement of the club funds when called upon by the club.

*Article No. 8*

The duties of the Executive Board shall be:

To act for the club in all matters ordered by the club.

To make final decisions upon member expulsions.

To properly investigate and present to the club all business or important activity situations.

To have a general control over club affairs.

Six members shall comprise a quorum of the Executive Board.

*Article No. 9*

The duties of a Road Captain shall be:

To plan all club tours, runs and other activities.

To lead the club in formation riding or parades.

To arouse interest in activities.

To enforce all rules of group riding.

To select one or two assistants to aid in special tasks.

*Article No. 10*

The duties of the Referee shall be:

To have general supervision over all sanctioned competition events promoted by the club. (The duties of Referee are outlined in the A.M.A. Competition Rule Book.)

*Article No. 11*

All elective offices shall be filled at an annual election to be held on _____ of each year and all officers shall hold this office for one year, or until their successors are elected and qualified.

*Article No. 12*

The regular meetings of the club shall be held on _____ at _____ P.M., but the President or Executive Board may call a special meeting at any time by posting a notice on the Bulletin Board at least four days in advance.

*Article No. 13*

_____ active members in good standing shall constitute a quorum for the transaction of club business.

This constitution may be amended or added to, the proposed amendment being submitted in writing at a regular meeting. It shall then be posted on the bulletin board for _____ weeks and voted upon at the next meeting. A two-thirds vote of all active members in good standing shall be required to pass an amendment.

*By-Laws*

No. 1.    *Robert's Rules of Order* shall govern the parliamentary proceedings of this club, unless otherwise provided for in these By-Laws. The order of business shall be:

1. Roll call
2. Reading of minutes of previous meeting
3. Report from officers
4. Unfinished business
5. New business

No. 2.    The standing committees of the Club shall be a House Committee of three members and a Tour Committee of three members. The House Committee shall have supervision of the Club House and be directly responsible for the maintenance of order, and the keeping of the Club furniture and fixtures in good condition. The Tour Committee, with the Road Captain as acting Chairman, shall have general charge of all Tours and Runs, subject to such orders as the club may give.

No. 3.    The Club dues shall be $_____ per month and the initiation fee $_____. The dues for each current month shall be paid not later than the 15th. Any member two months or more behind in his dues shall be considered not in good standing and shall not be entitled to vote at Club meetings.

No. 4.    All bills must be checked and approved by the Executive Board before they are paid. All checks should be countersigned by the President.

No. 5.    Applications for membership must be recommended by two active members of the club in good standing. Upon payment of dues, the applicant will be placed on probation for one month. At the expiration of that time, his conduct being satisfactory, he becomes a member and is entitled to all of the privileges of the Club.

No. 6.    Only active members shall be eligible to hold office in the Club.

No. 7.    Any member who is over six months behind in his dues, may be expelled from the club by a two-thirds vote of those present at any meeting.

No. 8.    A member may be expelled for conduct unbecoming a member of the club, but charges must first be made in writing and the accused member given a hearing before the Executive Board. The Executive Board shall take evidence and report its findings to the club with a recommendation that the charges be considered as proven and the accused member expelled, or the charges be considered not proven and the accused member remain a member of the Club. The Club shall thereupon take a vote to decide whether or not the recommendations of the Executive Board shall be adopted. It shall require a two-thirds vote of the active members present and entitled to vote to veto the recommendation of the Executive Board.

No. 9.     All active members of the Club shall be members of the A.M.A.

No. 10.     Amendments to the adopted constitution and by-laws may be added, provided that such in no way supercede or contradict the constitution and by-laws of the parent body, the A.M.A.

*Note: This chapter was prepared with the cooperation of the A.M.A.*

Chapter 7

# *CHOOSING THE RIGHT TOOLS*

THE TOOL KITS that are standard with most motorcycles are designed solely for emergency, trouble-shooting situations. At best they include a couple of wrenches, a spark plug socket and a screw driver. For regular repairs and maintenance you need a broader choice of equipment.

The best tools are drop-forged, a process that makes them rugged and dependable. The process is usually indicated on the tool; if you don't see it, chances are that the tool is not as well made as it could be. Many people think the best tools are sold only by large hardware stores and automotive jobbers, but there are several other sources. Some of the finest are sold by Sears, Roebuck and Company (with a good replacement guarantee). And Snap-on tools equally reliable, are sold from mobile salesrooms.

If you want to repair, service or hop-up motorcycles, a basic tool set should include three or four wrenches, two pairs of pliers, two screwdrivers, assorted drills and files and a set of feeler gauges. As you can afford to add specialty tools, buy items such as snap ring pliers, ring compressor and a torque wrench. Happily a good set of tools can be assembled slowly, and happily you can rely on good tools to last for years.

## Wrenches

There is hardly a process in motorcycle mechanics that doesn't require at least one wrench. You'll use them for tightening and loosening nuts and bolts. Wrenches are commonly classified by the design of their working end:

1. box end          3. combination
2. open end         4. socket
            5. adjustable

Start your set with either a box or open-end type. Both are nonadjustable and can be purchased individually or in sets. An average set contains five to 10 wrenches and costs less than 20 dollars. Box ends are so named because they "box" or enclose the nut or bolt head. They are the safest of all types, the least likely to slip. The wrench has 12 notches arranged in a circle (it's called a 12-point wrench) and one advantage of the design is its workability in restricted quarters. The handle can be used with only 15 degrees rotation. Other wrenches may need three or four times that scope. But even so, box wrenches are considered "slow."

By comparison open-end types are "fast." They have a three-sided slot and an open end that lets you slide the wrench quickly off and on. They are designed for "backing off" bolts after initial loosening with a box end. (However, it is fair to note that backyard mechanics generally use box and open ends interchangeably without regard for the niceties.) The wrenches have working ends of differing sizes so that one shaft actually contains two wrenches. A combination wrench has a box-end type on one end and an open-end version on the other. The two wrenches are of identical size, designed for "slow" and "fast" work.

Socket wrenches are made in two parts. They offer the reliability of a box end and the speed of an open end. The concept reduces cost since one handle can fit a range of sockets. A variety of handles are available but if you can buy only one choose a ratchet mechanism, since it both speeds things up and lets you work in tight quarters.

Adjustable wrenches are similar to open types, but one jaw is fixed and the other is movable. The size of the opening varies and you should choose one that fits the range of nuts and bolts on your machine. Always place the wrench on the nut so that the pulling force is applied against the stationary jaw and not against the adjustable segment. When used correctly an adjustable wrench can withstand considerable force. Special adjustable wrenches include stillson (for plumbing) and monkey wrenches. Neither are used on bikes.

While wrenches come in a variety of types, they also come in three measurements—American, Whitworth and metric. The choice depends on your cycle. American machines use American Standard wrenches. British bikes use Whitworth and Continental and Japanese bikes use metric types. The difference in the wrenches lies in the way they are measured. American types are measured in fractions of an inch, the distance taken across the parallel sides of the bolt head. Whitworth (also called British Standard) measurements are made at the shank. Metric measurements are made in a way similar to American types, but the dimensions are in millimeters.

If your bike can use an American Standard set, consider ordering enough wrenches so that some will fit the family car as well (providing it is U.S. made). Consider a set of from ¼ to $1\frac{3}{16}$ inch in intervals of $\frac{1}{16}$th inch. If you need metric types, 10, 12, 14, 17, 19 and 22mm will generally fit all of the bolts on a cycle. For Whitworth types order a set of five to ten wrenches (available from Sears, Webco, Hap Jones, Flanders and others).

If you buy socket wrenches you must consider both the socket size (which may be American, Whitworth or metric) and the "drive" size, that is the size of the square "finger" at the head of the handle. It fits to a female end on the socket. A quarter-inch drive is the smallest normally used for light mechanical work and a ⅜-inch drive is better. A half-inch version is generally too bulky and costly for cycle work.

## Pliers

The term "pliers" covers a surprising range of tools. It is important to have a good selection on hand to meet common situations. Never use pliers for tightening or loosening nuts and avoid using them on a hardened surface, which can dull their teeth and cause them to loose their grip. In the beginning consider these types of pliers:

*Slipjoint.* An elongated opening in the pliers body allows the jaw opening to be changed. The simplest types offer two or three positions and the more complex may offer four, six or more. Good pliers should have sharply milled teeth and it is important to check their condition before you buy. Pliers are made in various sizes and their overall length in inches determines their advertised size. Combination types are generally sold in lengths from five to ten inches.

*Longnosed.* Thin, rounded jaws that taper to a point are typical of longnosed pliers. They are ideal for lightweight shaping and bending and can be used in tight quarters. Again, the pliers should have sharp, well-defined serrated teeth. Occasionally longnosed versions will have cutting edges as well.

*Diagonal.* Sometimes called "dikes," diagonal pliers are made for cutting. They come in various sizes and are designed to handle wire and cotter pins but not sheet metal. Five- and six-inch diagonals are good for most cycle work.

*Locking.* Add a pair of locking pliers when you can. These have a cam action center and a bolt at the handle to let you adjust the jaw opening. One handle toggles over center to lock firmly against the object you want to grasp. An 8-inch pair has an opening of approximately 1¼ inches and a 10-inch version opens to about 1¾ inches.

As you expand your shop consider adding other special pliers: ignition and distributor pliers (about 5 inches long) and hog-ring and snap ring pliers (for removing various rings).

### Screwdrivers

You should have at least two screwdrivers, a plain tapered-tip type and a Phillips version. It may be necessary to have more than one of each. When using a driver with a tapered tip, a force is created through the taper, which tries to push the end of the tool out of the slotted screw head. It is best to have several tapered drivers so you can use the largest possible tip to counteract this action. The Phillips type is made with a specially shaped head to fit the unique cross-slotted Phillips screws. You will need two or three sizes to fit most of the screws on bikes. Ratchet screwdrivers have a drill-like chuck and adjustable tips. They can use both tapered and Phillips ends and if you like the idea, use them. I will admit to a prejudice against ratchet types.

## Hammer

Still a basic, primitive striking tool, hammers have been sophisticated into various types and sizes. You will probably need two, a ball peen and a soft-face hammer. The ball peen is a mechanic's all-around tool and is to the metal worker what the claw hammer is to the carpenter. By definition the word "peen" refers to indenting and to the side of the hammer head which does that work. Ball peens are made in several sizes up to 2½ pounds.

Soft-face hammers are to be used when you can't leave indentations or a trace of blows. Several types are available. Most have renewable tips of rubber or plastic but some have a clamp device which accepts rawhide or lead.

## Cold Chisels

Used for cutting and chipping, they are made of the highest quality tool steel. One end has a hardened cutting edge and the other a flattened, rounded hitting head. You can use chisels on any metal softer than that from which they are made, in short, any metal you can easily cut with a file. Chisels are made in various points, cape, diamond, round, and flat configurations are the most common. It is important to choose the proper point for the job at hand.

Use a flat-pointed chisel for flat work such as re- moving rivets or segments of flat metal. When you must cut in channels, grooves or square corners choose a cape-point with specially narrowed end. To cut round and circular grooves use a round-nosed chisel and use a diamond version for V-grooves and square corners. To avoid accidents keep the head of the chisel and the face of the hammer clean. In use hold the chisel firmly by its stock, that portion of its body above the cutting edge, yet hold it loosely enough to reduce the shock of each hammer blow.

### Files

When choosing a file consider first the type of teeth and their coarseness and then the file's length and shape. It is the combination of these characteristics that adapts a file to its jobs.

Common files have either single or double-cut teeth. The difference lies in the diagonal of the grooves. A single-cut file has diagonal grooves across the face of the file: a double-cut type has double grooves which criss-cross. When the grooves "water-fall"—that is, continue across the edge—you have a file with a "workable edge." When there is no waterfall you have a "safe edge"—that is, the file can be used without an edge inadvertently cutting material. A single-cut file always does a smoother job than one with double-cut teeth, but within the two categories you can buy files with three degrees of coarseness (graduating from rough to smooth): bastard, second-cut and smooth-cut.

The files are sold in many shapes from pillar to half-round and square. Let your dealer help choose the proper shape for each job. A choice of mill or pillar, taper and round styles will handle the majority of projects.

In addition, files are offered in a variety of lengths to 18 inches. Generally, the longer the file, the coarser its teeth, even though the file may be the same grade as a shorter one. Whatever file you buy if you will follow these rules you can be certain of quality work:

1. Equip every file with a handle. These must be purchased separately.

2. Files are designed to cut only on the forward stroke. Never pull a file backward across work.

3. Keep your body stationary; let your arms do the filing.

4. Clean the work area often and keep the file free of metal chips.

5. Store files individually to keep them sharp.

6. If a file becomes greasy or oily, clean it immediately. Never use one with an oily surface.

| Other tools | Approx. cost |
|---|---|
| Allen wrench set | $ 1.00 |
| Caliper, dial-type | 30.00 |
| Chain breaker | 4.00 |
| Drill, ⅜-inch chuck, electric | 40.00 |
| Drill bits, set | 7.00 |
| Gauge, feeler | 2.00 |
| Hacksaw | 3.00 |
| Magnet, pencil | 1.00 |
| Ring compressor | 7.00 |
| Pliers | |
|     Needle nose | 4.25 |
|     Cutter | 4.25 |
|     Regular | 4.00 |
|     Adjustable lock | 4.00 |
|     Vice-grip | 2.50 |
| Puller | 10.00 |
| Wrenches | |
|     Metric 6 pc set | 10.00 |
|     Sockets ⅜ drive | |
|         9 pc set | 5.30 |
|         92 pc set | 60.00 |
|     Torque | 10.00 |
| Soldering gun | 10.00 |
| Tin snips | 5.00 |

Vice (with replaceable steel faces)
    Jaws open to 5 in. .................. 39.00
    Jaws open to 7 in. .................. 60.00
    (With adjustable swivel base add $15.)

Chapter 8

## TROUBLE SHOOTING AND MAINTENANCE

### Ways to Keep Your Bike Running Longer and Better

ALMOST EVERY MECHANICAL PROBLEM—from an engine that refuses to start to one that overheats or runs roughly—has a cause that can be found and repaired economically. It is important to discover the cause as quickly as possible since speedy repairs add to the life of any bike. An experienced cycle owner will establish a logical system of investigation to find the problem with the least amount of effort. You should do the same.

There are many ways to trouble-shoot a problem cycle and the sequences below are only a few of the possibilities. Mechanical variations between two- and four-cycle designs make it impossible to include all of the probabilities, and in the procedures we've listed below some may be applicable only to two- or four-cycle engines.

### BASIC ENGINE PROBLEMS

1. **Engine runs poorly after starting.**
   *Probable causes:* Bad spark plug, defective coil,

improper carburetor mixture or improper float level.

*Repair procedures:* Check the spark plug. If the electrode is wet or sooty, or the gap incorrectly adjusted, correct the condition, replace the plug and try the cycle. If the plug is overheated, replace it with one of a lower heat range. If the plug seems good, check the ignition coil. Replace the coil if defective. If coil and plug are good check the carburetor float level. Adjust when necessary.

If the engine misfires at lower speeds as under acceleration, check carburetion closely. Examine the idle mixture; it may be richer than required. A clogged air cleaner is also a possibility, as is water or condensation in the carburetor float bowl itself.

If the engine dies as the throttle is opened the problem is one of carburetion. Be certain the idle speed is set high enough. The carburetion system may be overly rich or the choke lever may not be opening the choke completely.

**2. Engine overheats.**

*Probable Causes:* Improper fuel-air mixture, improper ignition timing, fouled or dirty plug, wrong chain tension or lubrication, carbon deposits in combustion chamber, low level or improper grade of oil, contact breaker point gap wrong, points dirty or burned, wrong plug heat range, clogged exhaust port.

*Repair procedures:* Remove the spark plug and check the electrode. If wet or sooty, clean, replace and try the engine. If the carburetor continues to foul, plug check the carburetor. Check chain and adjust if too tight or lubricate if necessary. Check the contact breaker points, adjust or replace if necessary. If all else seems to be working properly remove the head. Check the combustion chamber. If the head shows carbon buildup, clean.

Be sure to check the fuel-oil mixture. Insufficient oil (or the wrong grade) are common causes. A lack of oil via an automatic metering system is also a common problem. Similarly, a carburetor set too lean may cause the symptoms.

On many bikes retarding the ignition will help. Be sure to check the spark plug. The plug may be of the wrong heat range. Check the compression. If it is abnormally high suspect carbon buildup. A similar signal: when the engine "runs on" after the ignition is turned off. In each case remove the head and clean. It is possible to overload the engine, as when riding double, and occasionally the cooling fins are at fault. If they are caked with mud adequate cooling is nearly impossible.

### 3. Engine starts but will not run.

*Probable causes:* Out of fuel, clogged fuel valve or line, plugged vent hole in gas cap, inadequate oil level, carburetor damaged, connecting tube from carburetor to manifold leaks air or is damaged. See also Problem 1.

*Repair procedures:* Check fuel tank level, check position of three-way valve. It should be in "on" or "res" positions. If there is fuel and valve is properly set, check fuel lines and then gas cap and oil level. If the carburetor seems good, check the manifold tube before investigating the carburetor itself. In some cases, when all else checks out, ignition problems can cause similar symptoms.

### 4. Contact break points pitted or burned.

*Probable causes:* Improper timing, defective condensor, points covered with oil.

*Repair procedures.* Check the condensor first. Dirty terminals or a loose connection can cause ignition problems. If you cannot test a condensor, either replace with one known to be good or have it checked by your dealer. If the condensor is bad, replace it. If it is in good condition check ignition timing and adjust as required. Also replace contact breaker points with a new set.

5. **Engine does not start.**

   *Probable causes:* Carburetor, ignition system, spark plug, condensor, contact breakers.

   *Repair procedures.* Check fuel tank for gas and check the three-way fuel valve. Check fuel lines (one may be clogged or broken) and check the fuel tank vent cap. The vent could be clogged. Make an ignition check before investigating the carburetor needle valve, float level, etc. Remove the spark plug, attach the ignition wire cap then ground the plug against the head. Rotate the starter. If the spark is not strong or if there is none, the plug itself may be at fault. Check the electrode. If it is wet or sooty, clean, check the gap then replace. Try the engine. If it fails to start check the breaker points. Be sure the gap is correct and that the points are neither pitted nor burned. Trouble may also lie in a short, possibly in the coil or wiring. There may even be a problem at the starter switch. If the engine starts or seems to want to start, but will not continue to run, the problem may be one of three things: carburetor air-screw adjustment opened wide, carburetor gasket damaged, or choke opened too wide. If all else seems in working order check engine compression. See Problem 6.

**6. Engine will not start for lack of compression.**

*Probable causes:* Cylinder head gasket blown, valve tappet stuck open or clearance is incorrect (when an engine has valves), a foreign object is stuck between the valve and valve seat, excessive wear in cylinder walls or piston ring, ignition timing wrong.

*Repair procedures.* Check the easy possibilities first: Inspect the ignition timing, then dismantle the engine. Compression problems occur infrequently but are generally serious. To compare the compression in your cycle with recommended ratings use these commonly accepted figures. The amounts are the minimums for two stroke engines:

| Engine Size | Recommended Compression |
|---|---|
| 50cc | 100psi |
| 80cc | 100psi |
| 90cc | 100psi |
| 125cc | 112 to 130psi |
| 250cc | 135 to 155psi |

If the compression figures fall approximately 25 percent below these figures a ring job or major repair is probably required. To check, screw a compression gauge into the spark plug hole, or hold it firmly if it is an automatic type, then kick the starter two or three times with the throttle open.

**7. Engine stalls or stops after running.**

*Probable causes:* Out of fuel, clogged fuel line or valve, dirty spark plug, improper ignition timing, blown fuse, inadequate carburetor mixture.

*Repair procedures:* Check fuel level, then disconnect fuel line to check the flow. If adequate, check other factors. Also check fuses. Replace if blown.

On many cycles pilot lamp will not work with blown fuse.

Check the battery system. Be sure all connections are clean. Check the spark plug. It may be of the wrong heat range or may be sooty or wet. Clean, adjust or replace. Check the ignition timing and correct if required. Improper ignition timing can be a cause of hard-starting. Often it may be due to wear on the cam fiber. Check the capacitor and replace if points are burned or discolored. Both are signs of a faulty condensor. If points are badly worn, discolored or pitted, clean and dress them or if possible replace them with a new set. If the engine loses power at a specific throttle opening regardless of rpm the cause is probably poor carburetor or a worn or inadequate needle. But if the stalling occurs at various rpms the cause is commonly the ignition system. Check all parts of the system, points, plugs, high tension leads, connections, battery—everything. There is no way to uncover the cause except by a thorough examination.

But if the engine misfires under a load, yet regains its power when you gear down, the trouble may go something like this: plug, air cleaner or carburetor jet. Check the plug first. It may be breaking down from overheating. Possibly the plug has an improper heat range. Check the air cleaner carefully. If it is dirty, clean thoroughly. The carburetor main jet could be larger than required, its over size creating an improper pressure drop at wider throttle openings. At relatively lower speeds the over size results in an improper mixture. Tuning and replacement can solve the problem. Also check the timing. Spark timing becomes increasingly critical as the load increases.

If the engine misfires at higher speeds suspect

the main jet. It is responsible for the mixture controls. An improper float level is also a possibility, especially when set so that there is an inadequate amount of fuel in the bowl. The capacitor may be at fault; and often is on an AC magneto system. Poor capicators may perform adequately at lower speeds and yet can break down at higher rpms. If you cannot have it checked replace with one known to be good. Also check the high tension leads. Be sure there are no points at which the leads may leak.

## 8. Inadequate engine rpm.

*Probable causes:* Carburetor adjustments, dirty air cleaner, clogged fuel passage, defective spark plug, improper ignition timing. In rare cases troubles may include low battery or a mechanical condition such as bad rings, clogged ports or leaking gaskets.

*Repair Procedures:* If the fuel passage is clogged the spark plug will be dry, obviously dry. Replace the spark plug and clean the fuel passage. If the engine seems to stumble or not develop proper low speed rpms yet seems to run well at higher rpm, the trouble may be caused by carburetion, a wrong needle adjustment, a wrong idle setting or other problem. The spark advance may be set wrong. If the problem seems to clear itself once you run the cycle at high speeds the problem may simply be a "blowing out" of carbon or excess fuel.

If the problem develops at high speeds and if the engine seems to "peak out" so that you need to shift down, often the trouble may also be in carburetion or in the air cleaner. If the air cleaner is clogged an engine cannot breathe sufficiently to develop proper rpm. Ignition timing and cleanliness are also common causes. Be sure to check the spark plug and wiring from the distributor to the plug. If your cycle is small, say a 50 to 90cc, be sure you are not simply asking too much of the machine. An overloaded bike may simply not have enough horses for the job asked of it.

**9. Poor Idle**

(Also shows as slow response to throttle "snapping", poor performance at slow speeds, poor speed transitions.)

*Probable causes:* Improper air screw adjustment, throttle screw adjustment wrong.

*Repair Procedures:* Turn the air screw to a fully closed position. Back off the screw 1¼ to 2 turns then start engine and try quarter turns plus or minus this setting until the engine runs smoothly. Or back the throttle screw off completely, then turn in until the correct rpm adjustment is obtained.

If the intermediate speed seems wrong the jet needle may be improperly set. Check factory specifications, then adjust needle. The fuel level may also be wrong. The right jet needle setting will also correct this condition. When the high speed performance is poor the problem is generally a loose or dirty main jet, a clogged air vent tube or an improper choke adjustment. If the main jet is at fault remove, clean, install and adjust; then tighten properly.

**10. Generally poor performance.**

*Probable causes:* Improper ignition timing, poor carburetion, spark plug trouble, clutch, poor engine condition.

*Repair procedures:* Check the timing carefully. Adjust or correct as required. Check carburetor for proper mixture. It may be excessively lean or rich.

Both conditions can be checked by an examination of the spark plug and the exhaust stack. Check the plug to see if it is of the proper range and that the electrode is neither fouled nor dirty. Clean or replace if required. In rare cases a slipping clutch may cause similar symptoms. If all else seems good, check the general mechanical condition: factors such as compression, gaskets and rings. If the bike has high mileage an overhaul may be in order. Be sure the wheels turn freely. Occasionally the brake may be improperly adjusted or the chain may be set too tightly. Worn wheel bearings may also create similar symptoms.

11. **Cycle steers hard or pulls to one side.**
*Probable causes:* Bent steering stem, overtightened cone race, damaged steering balls, loose bearing front or rear, bent rim, wheel cushions not balanced, misalignment of cushions, bent fork.
*Repair procedures:* In all cases readjust or replace the worn or damaged parts. Check all items to rule out "good" and "workable" components.

12. **Clutch slips or is out of adjustment.**
*Probable causes:* Worn or warped clutch plate, lack of spring tension, worn or warped friction disc, uneven spring tension.
*Repair procedures:* In all cases repair, replace or adjust the part or parts.

## AUTOMATIC OILERS

The introduction of automatic oilers was an important improvement in two-stroke motorcycle design and while the systems are quite reliable they should be checked often. The most common problems are improperly adjusted control cables, air locks, bubbles and pump failures.

### 13. Inadequate oil delivery.

*Probable causes:* Bubbles (in the oil) are most commonly created in the pump case itself.

*Repair procedure:* Bleed the oil pump then check these areas for leaks: pump case, suction pipe connections, breather gasket, distributor oil seal, plug, pump case cover and plunger terminal.

### 14. Plunger will not work.

*Probable causes:* In some cases the distributor or starter plate will rotate. Check for a worn or clogged guide groove (for the plunger cam guide pin) and check the adjust-pully guide. The pin may be missing.

*Repair procedures:* Repair or replace part. In many cases the pump case cover will need replacement. In rare cases the pump itself will need repair or replacement.

### 15. Pump will not work.

*Probable causes:* Clogged pin hole, defective worm wheel pin, worn pin hole, improper or worn return spring.

*Repair procedures:* Clean pin hole, replace work part.

### 16. Distributor rotates with difficulty.

*Probable causes:* Plunger cam oil seal fits improperly or worn wheel plate is improperly adjusted.

*Repair procedures:* Refit the oil seal or replace if necessary, adjust wheel plate according to factory specifications. Also check guide grooves for plunger cam guide pin. In some cases these can be worn or clogged.

## 17. Improper pump setting.

*Probable causes:* Worn or defective plunger cam, worn or defective adjust-pully cam.

*Repair procedures:* Check cable control to the adjust-pully. The fitting should be set at factory specifications. Particularly check the clearance between the adjust-pully and the pump case cover. Clearance may be excessive. In some cases there may be excessive end play in the cable. In all cases set to factory specifications.

## 18. Adjust-pully will not move to contact the cam area.

*Probable causes:* Improper adjustment or fitting of parts or excessively tight fit between pump case and adjust-pully.

*Repair procedures:* Check fittings and make adjustments if possible. If adjustments cannot be made replace with new parts.

## OTHER PROBLEMS

*Unusual noises and vibrations.* The noises which develop in a two-stroke engine are different from those you'll find in a four-stroke version. Generally they change in accordance with engine load, rpm and road conditions and may be continuous or intermittent. In all cases check abnormal noises as quickly as possible. They may be the result of improper clearances but in some instances can be traced to symptoms described and diagnosed above.

By contrast excessive vibrations are nearly always traced to loose, worn or broken motor mounts. Exceptions can be found in mini-bikes. Check all mounting points thoroughly and repair broken areas or replace mounts if needed. Other causes may include poor timing, improper clutch adjustment and worn crankshaft. These are easily traced via the symptoms described.

## MAINTENANCE

There are several ways of measuring an engine's power. On one hand you can measure horsepower and on another torque. Such factors as piston displacement, compression ratio and compression pressures count. In one way or another all are measurements of engine efficiency.

### Brake or developed horsepower.

The measurement is relative and engine output is measured via a braking device. The measurements can be taken at various points. In addition the formula does not take into consideration differences in engine stroke and a power plant with a long stroke can provide a longer power stroke (and thus more horsepower) even though it will not show in the final ratings.

### Rated horsepower.

Rated horsepower is obtained by taking the bore of an engine in inches multiplied by itself then multiplied again by the number of cylinders divided by 2.5. The answer, still used occasionally for licensing purposes, is misleading. Rated horsepower is used more for automobiles than motorcycles.

### Indicated horsepower.

A rating seldom seen out of the laboratory, it is actually a measurement of the force delivered by the expanding gas to the cylinder itself. It is an esoteric figure and does not take into consideration such things as frictional losses. If you see it in a brochure, forget it.

### Drive, rear-wheel or "usable" horsepower.

Generally reliable measurements of an engine's usable power, most often made with a prony brake or dynamometer. Dynamometer readings are most common and the dynamometer is a device which creates a resistance (such as an electric armature revolving within a magnetized field or a paddle wheel revolving within a fluid) to absorb the energy. The engine is connected to the dyno while gauges register the power produced.

### Torque.

In addition to the various horsepower ratings, another measure of engine efficiency is torque, literally a twisting or turning effort. It is not so much a function of speed as it is of other engine characteristics and after a short rise in speed, torque may actually fall off. When torque is reduced at higher rpm's it is commonly the result of the engine's inability to obtain the same full charge of fuel it does at lower speeds. This is a function of factors such as volumetric efficiency and breathing.

Torque is measured in foot-pounds, a measurement of effort exerted at a distance of one foot from the center of rotation.

### Volumetric efficiency.

When an engine develops maximum torque at a specified rpm, say 2000 rpm, it simply means that the engine has its best volumetric efficiency at that speed, or, to put it another way, that the engine breathes best at that rpm. The maximum amounts of fuel and air are being drawn into the combustion chamber, burned and utilized to the best advantage. At higher rpm less mixture is drawn into the engine because of the increased friction of the gas itself and because the amount of time allowed for filling has been reduced.

With these factors in mind take time to read the horsepower curves for all cycles that interest you. If the power curve rises slowly in the lower end and then moves smartly to develop maximum power within a narrow range, 1000 to 1500 rpms for example, the engine could be designed for racing.

And when an engine gives maximum power at a very high rpm lasting only over a short range, the chances are the engine is "cammy"; that is, fitted with a special cam to concentrate its power at high speeds. The engine probably develops very little power at lower rpms and is not for general use. It may even be difficult to start. Buy an engine with a curve that reveals a steady rise in power from low rpms through the medium end. That chart usually indicates a versatile street/trail machine.

*Carburetion.*

Raw gasoline will burn, but not well enough to propel a motorcycle. To be combustible in the sense that an internal combustion engine requires it demands that the fuel be vaporized or mixed with air. The device which does this job is the carburetor. Early carburetors were crude and operated effectively only because the gasolines of those cycling days were also crude and vaporized easily. Today's fuels and motorcycles demand more sophistication.

While the carburetor is supposed to combine fuel and air in a suitable ratio for operation, there are many factors that make the job difficult. When an internal combustion engine is cold, as at starting, the fuel mixture must contain more than normal amounts of gasoline to run well. But when the engine begins idling it requires more air and when it reaches the preferred operating temperature it must use a mixture with even less fuel.

For normal operating conditions the best performance and economy is found in a mixture of 15 to 17 parts air and one part gasoline. For other effects, as for acceleration or top power, the mixture may need to be as rich as 12 parts air to one of fuel.

The air and gasoline are drawn separately into the carburetor by suction created by the piston. As it moves down the cylinder it creates a partial vacuum in the combustion chamber and cylinder and it is that difference in pressure (between the cylinder and the outside atmosphere) which causes the air to flow into the carburetor. The design of the carburetor itself makes the air draw fuel into its stream. A high degree of suction can be created in a line with moving air by reducing the size of the tube through which it flows at one point. The restriction is called a venturi and in a carburetor a tube or jet is placed precisely there. The suction at the venturi draws the gasoline into the air stream where it vaporized or mixed for use in the combustion chamber.

To operate properly the carburetor should hold a constantly level supply of fuel. If the fuel level is high too much fuel will be released and if the level is low an insufficient amount will be delivered. Most carburetors use a float in a reservoir (called the float chamber). Adjustments keep all factors operating properly.

The carburetors used on cycles can be divided into two groups, butterfly and slide, terms which describe the manner in which the air in the venturi is controlled. The slide is the most common type for cycles. Carburetors are further described as having a remote or concentric bowl or none at all. These terms refer to the float bowl position. Remote and "no bowl" are self-explanatory terms. A concentric bowl is centrally located and designed so that forces such as braking, acceleration and cornering do not affect the fuel level. The floatless or diaphragm type of carburetor is made to hold a minimum amount of fuel and is free of these problems.

The most famous cycle carburetor once was the British-made Amal. Now Japanese versions are more common. The best-known are Keihin and Mikuni. The Keihin is used on Honda cycles and the Mikuni on Yamaha types. Both are simple and effective when kept clean. Check carburetors often for dirt which can enter through the fuel as well as through the air. A major cause of overflowing on Amal-type carburetors is dirt beneath the needle valve seat.

Specifications for jet sizes and adjustments are found in your cycle manual. It is impossible to give the range required by the hundreds of cycles on the market. For example, a Yamaha YD3 uses a 120 main jet and 0.5 jet needle. The air screw turns out 1½ turns and the starter jet is a 60.

At high speeds the mixture ratio is adjusted by the main jet at three-quarters full throttle. If the engine runs smoothly when the throttle is backed off slightly it may mean the fuel mixture is too lean.

At medium speeds the mixture is controlled by the jet needle and the throttle valve at one- to three-quarter openings. To adjust the jet needle follow this procedure: There are five grooves in the upper part of the jet needle, counted from top to bottom. If the exhaust fumes are white the fuel mix is probably rich. Lower the jet needle one groove at a time. Do this by dropping the clip into the groove below the present setting. The standard setting for most YD3's is the third groove. If the engine does not run smoothly under load and if it feels as if the engine is being held back, the fuel mixture may be too lean. Raise the jet needle one groove setting.

At idle speeds the fuel mixture is controlled by the pilot air adjusting screw at settings between one-eighth and one-quarter throttle. Turn the idle screw completely in then back off six turns as a starting point. Adjust from then for the proper idle. The correct idle speed for most Yamaha machines is 200rpm.

Be sure to check the air cleaner on your machine often. Most cycles use a filter of one of these three types—wet metal, wet element or dry cartridge. The earlier wet mesh cleaners were more accurately air strainers with shredded metal centers soaked with oil. A basic trouble with them was the uneven size of the holes used to draw air into the carburetor. When an opening was small it filtered well, but when a hole was large it worked with less efficiency. Wet elements are not common today although a good version is still used on the Bultaco.

Dry cartridges are made of paper, fireproofed to prevent burning in case an engine backfires. The better versions work well, but the cheaper ones do not. As with metal types the hole size is critical. Dry filters with large holes will not filter properly and those with small holes may clog easily and restrict breathing.

*Maintenance and modification.*

Although a carburetor is probably the most reliable and trouble free item on an engine, it is the one part most tampered with. The carburetor is often blamed for problems not directly related to it.

Before adjusting any of the carburetor jets, check the fuel system carefully. Chances are the trouble can be solved there. Be sure there is fuel in the tank and that the fuel cock switch is properly set (is it on "stop" or "on" when it should be on "reserve"?). Then check the gas cap vent for dirt and the fuel lines for air. Water is still another possibility.

If you adjust the carburetor follow the directions in your owner's manual. Be sure to make changes only when the engine is running at normal temperatures.

Settings should not be made when the engine is cold. Be sure the throttle cable is properly adjusted at the hand grip. There is also a damper adjustment on some machines: both must be set properly and should be checked regularly. If your cycle has two carburetors remember that the engine will not run well unless they are synchronized. Normally this can be done by adjusting the cables so the two valves open as one.

The float level, inside the carburetor bowl, is adjustable. Each make (and sometimes model) requires a different fixed level. Normally the level can be changed by bending the float arm. If the float is set high there is excess gasoline and the bowl may leak, increasing the richness of the air-fuel mixture. When the level is low there is too little fuel and the motor may be difficult to start. It may even be impossible to make high and low-speed adjustments.

Modifications usually involve a change in the number or size of the carburetors. Most often the move is to larger ones (in venturi diameter) but if you plan such a switch be sure you are not overcarburetting. An engine with too much gas is really only good at high-speed drag racing. If you don't stick with stock carburetors, move up only one or two venturi sizes. In most instances a two-cycle engine will require a larger carburetor than a four-cycle of similar displacement. The two-cycle has a shorter filling time (on the intake cycle—generally 120 to 160 degrees of crankshaft rotation as compared with 250 or more degrees with a four-cycle).

Consider a switch to a smaller carburetor. A reduction in size may not be as crazy as it seems. It can deliver a cleaner low rpm pickup, which often means improved idling. Often two smaller carburetors will deliver better performance than one larger one. If you change a carburetor from a two-cycle to a four, plan for complete recalibration. The unit will run rich at all settings, partly because the jets are larger to allow for the increased passage of fuel in a shorter time and partly because the fuel itself can be thicker with lubricant mixed in it.

A complete induction system also includes the passageways from the carburetor to the combustion chamber, the ports which open into the chamber, and some provision for timing the entry of the fuel, sometimes by port position and sometimes with a rotary or reed valve. The modification of these areas requires substantially more engineering background than is considered basic for this chapter.

Chapter 9

## *A PLACE TO RIDE:*

## Ecology, Land Use and Trail Bikes

I MET FRED in the days when it was fashionable to ride wherever you wanted. He was a "boondocker," one of the best off-road riders in the West, and collected rough and rugged places to ride. I remember the day he ran to my house shouting, "I've found the greatest trail, steep, crooked and narrow. You'll never make it."

Of course we tried it, made the trail and came back to enjoy the challenge again and again. Then I lost track of Fred. I met him only a few days ago after a lapse of years. "Found any new trails?" I asked.

He shook his head. "I do other riding," he said. "I mean, how can you enjoy things like that now?"

Like Fred thousands of other cycle riders are taking a new look at our environment. They are asking if it is possible for motorcycles and open land to go together. Some ask me if there are really places where bikes can run without creating havoc. I tell them there are, but before I prove it, let's take a look at the problem.

Of course the basic trouble is population and consumerism. In the rest of the world: too many people. In the United States: too many people consuming too many things. The United States, with less than 6 percent of the earth's population, contributes more to the damage of our planet than any other country. In one short generation the people of Southern California have transformed their environment into a place where experts say man can no longer live a healthy existence. The story is being repeated across the country in air, land and water pollution.

Life depends on an eight-mile layer of air and we are dumping harmful gasses and foreign particles into this vital zone at an alarming rate. On the ground, timber, soil, mineral and wildlife resources are being used without thought of replacement. And man is adding pollutants to water faster than natural cycles can remove them.

Thankfully young people seem to understand the situation better than the older generation. They know we live in a closed space ship. They know our resources are limited. They know our priorities are distorted. They know we have not managed our supplies well. And they know we are headed for disaster. But they also know the situation can be reversed.

First, we must stop population explosions and pollution. Then we must revitalize areas that are failing and must plan ahead. Public officials now thoughtlessly build freeways across fertile, food-producing fields and erect buildings where parks should be. We need to reverse our sense of values.

Second, we need an aroused public. We need people armed with facts, able to make up their own minds. As Americans, we can get the kind of future we want only when we are willing to vote and pay for it. Our young people are beginning to become concerned, alarmed and active.

Then we need to consider recreation. We know little about man's need for open spaces, trees and wildlife or even much about the reactions he gets from them. Without facts it is difficult to talk realistically about man, his land or his vehicles.

Marion Clawson in his book, *Crises in Outdoor Recreation,* says, "Americans don't just *want* outdoor recreation: they *need* it. . . . As people we don't feel right unless we can get back from time to time to the out-of-doors. If we ever loose this urge there will have been a profound change in the national character. . . . Meeting the demand for such recreation is a national problem of the first rank." Clawson is the Director of Resources for the Future's Land Use and Management Program.

What Clawson has to say is as germane for off-road bike riders as for back packers and bird watchers. But there are social pressures against cyclists not felt by other outdoor users. People tell me I've abandoned all interest in our land because I own a motorcycle. Obviously, that is just not so. The motorcycle brings me close to the land. I am responsible. I do work constructively for a better environment. A majority of the riders I meet are doing the same. Progress is slow not because the riders are unconcerned, but because the problems are complex.

For example, there are shortages of land. It may seem improbable to speak of shortages when 283 million acres have been designated for public recreation and another 500 million are publicly owned although seldom used. But the essential acres are spread throughout 25,000 individual areas from National Parks to roadside rests, and the reserves are mostly in the west. We have 185 million potential outdoorsmen in the U.S. The popular areas, Yellowstone, Yosemite, Grand Teton and others are often full and if even half the potential users decided to go out on the same afternoon 25,000 recreational sites would be ridiculous. If the population continues to grow as projected in thirty years there will be even less room.

Obviously recreational land must be conserved and

used wisely. The two tenants are compatible with motor-cycles and the California desert is proof. It extends south through Death Valley 240 miles to the Mexican border and west from the Colorado River more than 100 miles to the fringes of Los Angeles. The area is challenging and exciting and an estimated 800,000 dune buggies, four-wheel drives, ATV's and motorcycles now explore it. Most owners use their rigs wisely, but some do not.

The environment is fragile, easily scarred, slowly healed and protected only by an inhospitality which modern off-road vehicles are breaking down. Some scientific, cultural and historical values have succumbed. The Giant Intaglio, a huge prehistoric drawing, has been nearly destroyed. The beautiful petroglyph at Inscription Canyon has been quarried. Some rare animals and fish are endangered. But it is obvious "Keep Out" signs can solve nothing.

Instead an Off Road Vehicle Advisory Committee was formed by the Bureau of Land Management last year with 15 members representing desert users (cattlemen, dune buggy drivers, four-wheel drive owners, cycle riders, rock hounds and others), conservationists (Sierra Club and Desert Protective Council), and Government agencies (California Department of Fish and Game and the BLM). The Committee studied the desert, its use and misuse, the problems and the needs of those who use it. They looked for ways land users could work together in harmony and ways in which the desert could be used but not abused. As a start ORVAC suggested that areas be classified in three groups:

*Open use areas*    All public lands are considered open to use by off-road vehicles until action is taken to restrict them. Open use areas are those where off-road vehicles are allowed with only minimal restrictions.

*Restricted areas* When conditions require, areas will be designated restricted. Restrictions could be seasonal, daily or periodical limitations, vehicle class limits or vehicle density ceilings. Use would be limited to prolong or protect the life of the land, plants or wildlife. There would be some vehicle use, but less than in open-use areas.

*Nonuse areas* Areas in which erosion or other destructive action, resource value or other consideration requires that off-road vehicles be prohibited. Vehicles would then be confined to the main access roads.

These regulations represent a start. The desert will be saved and vehicles will still use it, but each environment may need its own rules. What is workable in the desert may not prove functional in the mountains. We do not now have sufficient information for new answers. Those of you who are concerned should help.

Another solution was proposed by a rider who suggested that a National Monument in Southern California be opened to off-road rigs. The area has few paved roads and fewer camping areas. The fellow told me, "The dirt roads are of real interest only to four-wheel drives, dune buggies and cycles. All that is required is for the government to designate those roads as unsuitable for passenger cars. If they are made primitive trails, strictly for off-road vehicles, we've found a place to run. If the vehicles stick to the roads (and they will) open-use cannot contribute to erosion." The idea represents another sensible, practical possibility. But there are more. How many can you think of?

Private areas represent still another possibility. South of Los Angeles, Saddleback Park is a busy, popular place. It is a network of carefully planned trails set in acreage unsuitable for urban development, away from private housing and industrial developers, yet only an hour from Los Angeles. Riders flock there because the trails are challenging and the environment friendly.

In Simi, California, the solution may be a public area. There, motorcycles and mini-bikes were blamed for a host of headaches until cycle dealer Dick White stepped in with a two-stage plan. Working with city officials he helped pass a stiff ordinance prohibiting off-road riding within the city limits. Then, still working with city officials, he helped to obtain 100 acres adjacent to a county park. Cycles, mini-bikes and ATV's will be welcome. The area is still under development, but plans call for trails, a hill climb and even an oval track. Similar programs are under study by several cities. The Los Angeles Police Department, for example, is working to develop safe mini-bike areas.

In the end each community will have to develop its own solution. One may choose the "desert plan," another may prefer a private area like Saddleback and still another may choose a public center like Simi, but the final approach is not important. As long as the solutions include provisions for motorcycles and mini-bikes the plans are realistic. While law enforcement officials, motorcycle manufacturers, cycle dealers, bike owners and others work to develop ecologically sound places to ride, there are many things you can do:

1. *Follow regulations*    Stick to designated trails. Don't cross open land, but if you must, choose the best ground. Avoid marshes and marginal terrain. When you find "Closed Area" signs, obey them.

2. *If you think a closure order is unfair, argue later*
Not long ago BLM officials near Fresno, California closed the Panoche area because off-road vehicles refused to stick to a 15-mile loop set aside for running. One argument for the closure was that there were not enough BLM officials "to police the area." Many riders feel the closure wrong and are working to have Panoche re-opened. But it is obvious that those who disobeyed the original regulations helped to promote the closure. It is just as obvious anyone violating the closing now is making it more difficult to have the area reopened.

3. *Don't litter*   Don't dispose of beverage cans or bottles along a trail. If you see litter stop, pick it up. Carry out all refuse.

4. *Use a muffler*   It is neither necessary nor desirable to run open pipes. A reduced sound level makes more sense. In a forested area use a Forest Service approved spark arrestor.

5. *Don't break new ground*   You can have fun riding without tearing up new country. Don't climb virgin hills. Stick to approved areas. The time when a vehicle would accept the challenge of uncharted land is over. It is time to recognize it.

6. *Camp safely*   If you camp overnight eliminate pollution. Use biologically degradable soaps and other compounds and do not drain fuel or oil tanks in an effort to repair your bike. Leave a clean camp.

7. *Develop an ecological conscience*   Feel the character of the country around you. Read about the ecology and environmental problems. Find ways

to help. If you belong to a cycle club discuss the problems at meetings.

It is true that off-road vehicles can contribute to the problems of our environment, but eliminating vehicles is not the answer. In some cases damage is caused by irresponsible owners riding in an irresponsible manner and in other cases it is a matter of too many vehicles. In the west back packers and horsemen have polluted wilderness lakes and streams, not through carelessness, but through the force of numbers. Such problems can be solved.

For riders the rules outlined above are ecologically sound. If you follow these seven points you can ride with the knowledge that you are not a part of the problem, but a part of the solution. It is the sort of solution that concerned riders like Fred can live with—and that's good.

---

Four-wheel drive clubs have been using off-road areas in a responsible, organized manner for years and one thing that has brought the drivers together is their Code of Ethics. The points it makes are important and with a few changes in wording it is one we propose for cycle riders.

## OFF-ROAD CODE OF ETHICS

As Members of the American public who operate cycles to enjoy the awe-inspiring beauty of our mountains, valleys, deserts, forests, marshes, meadows and all other back country areas, we will:

**1.** Leave the land and its vegetation as we find it. Help to preserve plant life and soil by limiting travel to established roads and trails. Avoid cutting switchbacks and driving through most meadows which will leave permanent scars.

**2.** Protect the history of our nation by not disturbing old mining camps, ghost towns, diggings or other historical or natural values.

**3.** Respect the rights and property of other user groups such as miners, ranchers, fishermen, hunters and other recreationists.

**4.** Conduct all trips in a safe, sane manner.

**5.** Accept the responsibility of keeping the back country beautiful by packing out litter.

**6.** Give everyone we meet the courtesy of the road—safety and courtesy are contagious.

**7.** Observe local history, the geology of the land and the ecology of the vegetation so that we may more fully appreciate the splendor of our national heritage.

Chapter 10

## *TEN TOP RACES:*

### The 1971 Schedule, the Best Races to See, How to Get There, Where to Stay

THOUSANDS of motorcycle racing events are staged yearly. The AMA sanctions five thousand and a significant number are handled by other organizations. If you are a rider the action is all around and if you're a spectator, you are in real luck. Cycle racing is one of the greatest spectator sports. Which races should you see? "All of them" is the obvious answer, but barring that we've selected ten events. They represent a cross-section of the action, the best in each type of racing. See them and you'll know what motorcycle competition is all about.

400 sanctioned AMA events are Professional races. The remainder are Sportsmen events. The terms refer to two important categories of riders. Sportsmen are nonprofessionals, riders who compete only for points and glory. The Professionals are men who ride for a little of both glory and cash. There are three types of Professional riders. The first-year pro is a Novice. After one season and an accumulation of 40 points, a Novice becomes an Amateur. When he earns 80 points he becomes an Expert. Only Expert riders race in the National Championship circuits, but all AMA pro-

grams have Expert and Amateur events and some include Novice racing as well.

Racing cycles are current production bikes available in "adequate quantities" to the public. The rule insures that no factory can dominate the sport with special, high-cost machines no casual rider could afford. The engines and transmissions must be identical to those on production cycles, but modifications are allowed to frame, forks, brakes and suspension and engine "tuning" is permitted. Novices can ride machines to 250cc's; Experts and Amateurs can ride anything up to 750. The bikes must have handlebar control levers, footpegs, brakes and adequate tires and all must pass strict safety inspections.

Each rider is required to wear an approved helmet, goggles, leather pants and a long-sleeved coat. Boots must be at least eight inches high. Dirt racers wear an additional piece of protective gear, the "hot" or skid shoe, a steel plate worn under the sole of the left boot.

## Flags

A number of flags are used to signal riders on the track. Each has a different color or combination of colors and each has a special meaning. Racing is more fun when you know what the flags mean:

| | |
|---|---|
| WHITE | Start of the race |
| YELLOW | One lap to finish. White and yellow flags crossed means the race is half finished. |
| RED | Danger, but no "hold" on positions |

| | |
|---|---|
| BLACK | Extreme danger, hold position; disqualification; stopping of the race |
| WHITE WITH RED CROSS | Ambulance on track |
| WHITE WITH BLACK CENTER | Move over, another rider is trying to pass |
| BLACK AND WHITE CHECKERED | End of race. First bike flagged is winner. |

Racing covers a wide range of events, but five types contribute points to the Grand National Championship. All are great to watch, even though the action is different.

*Dirt track and Speedway*     Held on tracks at least one half mile in circumference. Dirt tracks are flat while speedways are banked. The length of the tracks vary and so do the events. "Half mile" races must be run longer than three miles but less than 15 for events other than national races. National half mile contests must have five-mile heats and ten-mile finals. "One mile" races must cover more than five miles, but less than 50. Speedway races can be as long as 200 miles with no minimum distance.

*Short track*     Held on tracks less than 2,250 feet in circumference. Similar to oval events, the sport is mostly centered in the Midwest and California.

*Tourist Trophy or TT*     Courses are of no specified length, but races cannot be held on travelled roads. Course should include right and left turns and possibly a hill. Riders must be forced to use gears and brakes during the event.

*Road race*     Held on a closed course, part of which

can be a public road. It should be of at least 50 miles duration and should duplicate, as closely as possible, regular road riding.

## 1971 Schedule

The new season includes seven road races, twelve half-mile events, four mile runs, five TT events and three short-track races in the National Championship circuit. The races are held from late January through mid-November. This year the events will pay a total of $380,000 in prize money—a record. At this writing approved dates for the season are incomplete, but include:

| | | |
|---|---|---|
| Jan. 29 | Houston, Tx | 20 Lap T.T. |
| Jan. 30 | Houston, Tx | 25 Lap S.T. |
| Mar. 14 | Daytona, Fla | 200 Mile R.R. |
| Apr. 25 | Atlanta, Ga | 125 Mile R.R. |
| May 2 | Cumberland, Md | 20 Lap ½ mile |
| June 5 | Louisville, Ky | 20 Lap ½ Mile |
| June 13 | Loudon, N.H. | 100 Mile R.R. |
| June 20 | Terre Haute, In | 20 Lap ½ Mile |
| June 27 | Columbus, Ohio | 20 Lap ½ Mile |
| July 5 | San Jose, Ca | 20 Lap ½ Mile |
| July 11 | Kent, Wn | 100 Mile R.R. |
| July 17 | Castle Rock, Wn | 30 Lap T.T. |
| July 24 | Ascot, Ca | 50 Lap T. T. |
| July 31 | Corona, Ca | 20 Lap ½ Mile |
| Aug. 8 | Livonia, Mi | 20 Lap 1 Mile |
| Aug. 13 | Santa Fe, Il | 25 Lap S.T. |
| Aug. 15 | Jennerstown, Pa | 20 Lap ½ Mile |
| Aug. 22 | Mt. Pocono, Pa | 100 Mile R.R. |
| Sept. 5 | Talladega, Ala | 200 Mile R.R. |

| Sept. 12 | Nazareth, Pa | 50 Lap 1⅛ Mile |
| Sept. 19 | Sacramento, Ca | 25 Lap 1 Mile |
| Sept. 25 | Ascot, Ca | 20 Lap ½ Mile |
| Oct. 3 | Oklahoma City, Okla | 20 Lap ½ Mile |
| Oct. 17 | Ontario, Ca | 200 Mile R.R. |

All of the events contribute important points toward the Grand National Championship, but some events are more important because they are worth more points (101 is the maximum) or because they pay greater prize money. These are the races we think you should see. This is our schedule:

*March 14    200 mile road race        Daytona, Florida*
After two races in January to work out the kinks, most riders are up for this one—the first big race of the season. Daytona pays a large purse and is worth 101 points. It is a "don't miss" race.

The track is near the Atlantic Ocean in North Central Florida, off U.S. 1. Motels are plentiful although reservations are recommended. If you like camping try Tomoka State Park, three miles north of Ormand Beach on the Old Dixie Highway, U.S. 1. In town try one of the six private trailer parks.

*May 16    Half mile            Jennerstown, Pennsylvania*
Although held early in the season, Jennerstown is a psychological race. By May the top riders are sorted out and the points are important. The race is an excellent example of the half mile event.

*June 12-13    100 mile road race        Loudon, N.H.*
A new version of the old Laconia Gypsy Tour, one of the best-publicized events on the calendar. There

used to be bike shows and other events before the 100 mile running, but an unfortunate incident in 1963 (involving an outlaw cycle group) caused the competition to be moved to Loudon. The races have never slacked and last year the track was paved and widened, increasing top speeds. Although the race is held early in the season, the winner traditionally places among the top ten riders.

To see the event, drive to Laconia then south 15 miles on highway 106. The nearest large town is Concord, one mile north of the junction of highways 89 and 93. Consider making your headquarters in one of the campgrounds around Lake Winnipesaukee, 20 miles north. Two of the popular ones are Gunstock, a county park at Balknap and Blake's Brook, south on highway 202. Gunstock has toilets and showers, but neither electricity nor sewer hookups for recreational vehicles. About 30,000 people come to Loudon for the event so make reservations early. For information write to Gunstock, Laconia, New Hampshire 03246 or Blake's Brook, Gossville, New Hampshire 03239.

*August 15    Tourist Trophy or TT        Peoria, Illinois*

Peoria is a traditional event drawing thousands throughout the Midwest. One TT race makes you an addict and this race has to be one of the best.

At TT's I hopefully watch Eddie Mulder, one of the top riders in the business. But last year at Peoria he had his thunder stolen by Jim Rice. Rice jumped to a substantial lead with Mulder second and Jim Corpe third. Other riders jockeyed for position lap after lap. Then Dave Aldana shot from the middle of the pack and slid into fourth behind Corpe. One more lap and he passed Corpe and Mulder taking second. Rice held his lead and the event finished that way. This year you can look for a fresh battle between Aldana and Rice.

The nearest public campground is 15 miles northwest of town, off U.S. 50 near Brimfield and most of the spectators stay in motels. The Chamber of Commerce will list the best ones for you. Write to them in Peoria, Illinois 61600. To get to the track follow either Interstate 80 or 55 to highway 74. The town bisects that highway.

*September 4-5 200 mile road race Talladega, Alabama*

Held near the end of the season and deep in the South, Talladega is probably the second most important race on the circuit. The 200 miler is worth 101 points, enough to keep a needy rider going toward the championship. For a man down in points, or money, this is a real pull-out-all-stops event.

Last year Gary Nixon dropped his bike in a fall at more than 100mph. He picked himself up in the outfield and began pushing his Triumph to start it when an excited fan leaped to the infield and helped. The push cost him the race, disqualifying him instantly. Talladega is like that. The competition is frightening—and the real winners are the spectators.

Camping is excellent in three private parks. You can make reservations by contacting: General Lee Marina and Campground, Route 1, Box 62, Cropwell, Alabama 35054; Holiday Park, Route 1, Cropwell, Alabama 35054; or Willimgham's Docks, Route 5, Talladega, Alabama 35106. If you prefer motels there are good ones in Birmingham, the state's largest city just 41 miles east.

Talladega is at the junction of state highways 21, 77 and 231 and each of these intersects a major freeway. The track is about 40 miles from Birmingham, about 120 miles north of Montgomery.

*September 16    Mile                Sacramento, California*

J. C. Agajanian's Sacramento race offers the highest-paid mile in the circuit. It is always a crowd pleaser. Gene Romero took the National Championship at Sacramento last year, two races before the end of the season—an unheard of accomplishment. Although chances of a repetition are remote (because of the addition of the Ontario road race later), Sacramento still looms large on the schedule.

The track is located in the old state fairgrounds, at the junction of two major highways—north and south Interstate 5 and east-west Interstate 80. The closest state park is at Folsom Lake, east of town. With 150 spaces the area offers good facilities. You can reach it off the Folsom-Auburn County Road, 12 miles south east of Pilot Hill. There are many excellent motels in town and reservations are not always required in September, but they are a good idea.

*October 17    200 mile road race    Ontario, California*

Perhaps this new race is the AMA's way of keeping the championship up for grabs until the very end. The Ontario event is new, now the last race of the season, and offers a smashing finish. It supplies 101 points and the richest purse in history—$50,000. So much is at stake that riders will put everything they have into winning. It has to be the race to see even if you miss all others.

The area is a difficult one for campers. It is close to Los Angeles with no open areas for "free" camping. There are plenty of hotels and motels, some inexpensive. In an area as heavily populated as this, reservations are not essential if you don't mind driving. But consider the traffic jams and try to stay close to the track. For information write to the Ontario Chamber of Commerce, Ontario, California 91761. Also try Riverside, Pomona and San Bernardino. All are close. October weather in Los Angeles is hot, hot, hot. Dress accordingly.

*Speed Week    Record Runs*                *Wendover, Utah*

Four hundred miles north of Reno, Nevada, I saw the skyline of Wendover, a series of one-story buildings punctuating the desert that had accompanied me since Reno. I was on my way to see the famed Speed Week on the Bonneville Salt Flats. Since I had lost my nickel to one of Bill Harrah's slot machines, I had expected to see some changes in the scenery, but mile after mile there had been nothing but sand, aromatic sage, chaparral pea and endless lengths of barbed wire.

There had been towns like Battle Mountain, Winnemucca, Elko and Wells. All with one story buildings as plain as the desert that surrounded them, as though their color had faded into the muted sand.

I sped up to see what the town was like. "Wendover," white painted rocks proclaimed from the hillside. Then over the ridge a tall neon cowboy gestured toward a casino. Beyond I could see it, like a great white ocean—the Great Salt Lake Desert.

At dawn they began coming with wierd, modified cars and bikes, brightly painted and on trailers. A line forms quickly at the registration booth and at the inspection station and old-timers catch up on the news. There is excitement and an anticipatory air even though none of the vehicles run. I open a beer and look around. From the starting line I can see for miles. Ahead is the ten-mile course. The sun is still low on the horizon but it is hot and a glare bounces off the salt, burning me from underneath. A man at the STP booth gives sun hats to racers and takes pity on me. He's a veteran of many Speed Weeks and wouldn't think of missing one now.

At one P.M. the first engine cracks to life and heads turn to see what it is. It's a black-framed special running two huge Harley 883's. A short, heavy man rolls it to the line and swings his leg away. His partner, a tall, painfully thin man with brown leathers, walks over and, bending to reach the clip-ons, guns the engine to a growl. He settles easily on the bike, the starter signals "any time," and he leaves the line. We watch. Now he is a black speck on the horizon, swallowed by the salt and the distance and all that is left is the sound, disappearing itself into space.

This is Bonneville. Pure racing. Some Big Names, some small. The competition is the clock and once you've come you know you will be back. The cycles and rods are exciting and the people are friendly, willing to talk at length about their machines. The weather is awful, hot, hot, hotter, and the races are exciting. All around are engines going *vroom, vroom,* and you wait to see them run.

The place is Bonneville on Highway 40 at the Utah-Nevada border. Wendover is five miles from the course. It has no campgrounds although Utah arranges a makeshift area. There are six motels in Wendover and reservations are recommended. A-1, Stateline and Western are the popular ones, but Patio, Wendover and Lewis Brothers are also good. Take your choice. Bring a hat, sunglasses and sun tan lotion. Wear light clothing and add a sleeved shirt for protection. Bring tennis shoes—the salt is easier on rubber than leather.

*Berkshire Trials*                    *Berkshire, Massachusetts*

You can rank this one as America's toughest enduro and because it is an international event, not sanctioned by the AMA, it has a unique feeling. You can't describe it, but there's a freedom here you don't see at many other events.

Middlefield, the race center, is in the northern portion of Berkshire County, located on a back road off Highway 7. Its just north of Alice's Restaurant in Stockbridge. There, the fairgrounds are taken over, the stock pens filled with bikes. The timing equipment is connected to the computer at the Massachusetts Institute of Technology.

The event pits man and machine against a treacherous countryside and tough, demanding trails. To win, a rider has to beat the land, not his fellow riders. The epitome of a Trials event is the ISDT, the International Six Day Trials. Teams come from all over the world to compete in it and to be chosen for the American team, a rider must do well here. That is what makes the event so important. By the time of Berkshire the Canadian team has been chosen and this event is their one important training session.

With competition of that caliber, the race is a "must-see" event. Yet it can be a difficult one for spectators unless you are willing to risk the rains that often come about this time. The run lasts two days. Last year 195 of the starting 400 riders completed the first day. Rains came during the night and on the second day only 43 were able to finish the race.

Camping is easy. There is often room at the fairgrounds and October Mountain, in nearby Lenox, offers room at a State Park. There are a number of good motels along U.S. 90.

*Baja, 500 and 1,000 mile races*          *Baja, Mexico*

Baja's two famous races have generated enough excitement to lure more than 200 contestants. Open to bikes and cars, the races are dusty, rugged and fun. It doesn't matter whether you ride or watch.

The route is easy enough to follow with a map. Both begin at Ensenada. The course is identical for several hundred miles. It leads south through Santa Tomas and Camalu (where the pavement ends) to San Quintin and El Rosario. Then it leads inland through Santa Inez and the dry lake at Rancho Chapala. The courses separate below the Rancho. The 500 leads north to the Gulf of California, Puero Citos and, finally, San Felipe. The 1000 continues south through El Arco, San Ignacio and other small towns to La Paz.

The two events are run at different times of the year so it is possible to see both. The 100, for example, is held the first week in November. Charter planes are available to take you over the riders, stopping at points along the way to watch the action from the ground, but there are drawbacks to air travel—not counting the expense. For one, you miss the camping and the countryside. I stick to the land, the action and Mexican hotels. You won't see all of the action, but you'll get the flavor of it and you will bring home memories to last for years.

A good spot to begin is at El Rosario, where food (especially good lobster omelets at Juanita's), lodging and excellent Mexican beer make the race pleasant. Another point for real action is at the dry lake bed at Chapala. There the land is covered by unbelievably fine silt, so thick you can't see the tracks of the vehicles ahead, and so fine it sprays into the air like thick clouds to reduce vision to inches and to cut the light to a dull gray. The silt rushes over you, sticking to your hood, your wheels, your face. If you are racing it is miserable, but if you are watching it is one of the most exciting points on the course.

Any good map of Baja will help you find your way,

tell you where to go and where to stop. *The Lower California Guidebook* by Gerhard and Gulick is still one of the best. Cliff Cross's *Baja California Mexico* features a number of new and accurate maps. It is available from Cross Guidebooks, North Palm Springs, California, at $3.50.

Driving beyond Ensenada and San Felipe requires a tourist card. If you are flying down, get yours from the airline before you leave the States. If you drive be sure to pick it up at the closest border town. No vaccination is required, but you will need a birth certificate or naturalization papers. Bring your U.S. driver's license and stop at the border (on the U.S. side) to buy Mexican automobile insurance. It is a must and can save days of trouble. Don't worry about money. Start out with a few small U.S. bills and in hours you will have all of the pesos you want.

Camping is the best part of your trip. There are no restrictions and all of Baja is one beautiful campground. Bring everything—water, food, campstove and fuel.

## FIM RACING

The international affiliates of the Federation Internationale Motorcycliste unanimously approved the entry of the American Motorcycle Association in the FIM as the sole representative in the U.S. The vote came recently in Cannes, France. It has been a long time developing and no matter how you feel about the AMA and MICUS, the simplicity of the decision is bound to be good for American racing.

The 81 FIM delegates representing 48 nations from all parts of the globe overwhelmingly approved the installation of the 120,000 member AMA into the world racing body. Support from Iron Curtain delegates, who form a strong bloc in the federation, was not expected. AMA officials said it can only be construed as a diplomatic endorsement which paves the way for an international exchange. It could bring a kind of motorcycling similar to the world Olympics.

As the sole FIM affiliate in the U.S., the American Motorcycle Association will be expected to manage and sanction a full program of international activity eventually including a U.S. Grand Prix which would award points toward world championships in road racing and motocross. This year the U.S. will run an eight-event Trans-Ama International Motocross series, a pilot project for the larger program which will follow. Racing in the Trans-Ama will be England's former FIM world champion, Jeff Smith, Sweden's Gunnar Lindstrom and the current World Champion, Belgian rider Joel Robert. For information on this or other events, contact the American Motorcycle Association, 5655 No. High Street, Worthington, Ohio 43085.

Chapter 11

## *1970 RECORDS:*

## A Short Library of Racing Records

IN A SPORT advancing as rapidly as motorcycling, speed
records are generally transient. The majority last less
than one year. The AMA establishes classes according to engine size, frame design and other classifications
and times and certifies all runs. The following records
were set at AMA sanctioned events and are current.

### BONNEVILLE

Bonneville records are straightaway top speed world's
records. The run is a measured mile distance and each
rider runs both ways.

The classifications are divided into three segments:
Frame, Engine, and Displacement classes.

*Frame Classes:*
  C    Stock frame—equipment meets standards for
       approved motorcycles.
  A    Modified frame—unlimited design, yet with no
       streamlining.
  PS   Partial streamliner stock frame—meets equip-
       ment standards for approved motorcycles with
       partial streamlining.*

* *Side view reveals entire front wheel and rider.*

APS Partial Streamliner modified frame—unlimited design, with partial streamlining.*

S  Fully Streamlined wheels covered—unlimited design, streamlined (separate compartment for engine, firewall between rider and engine, and fire extinguisher with engine controlled by rider).

All equipment must receive power transmission through the rear wheel only. A rear wheel brake is required.

*Engine Classes:*

C  Stock engine, gasoline—meets equipment standards for approved motorcycles.

AG**  Modified engine, gasoline.

A**  Modified engine, fuel.

AB**  Supercharged engine, gas or fuel.

*Displacement Classes (in cc's):*

| | | | |
|---|---|---|---|
| 50cc's | 200cc's | 600cc's | 883cc's |
| 100cc's | 250cc's | 650cc's | 1000cc's |
| 125cc's | 350cc's | 700cc's | 1200cc's |
| 175cc's | 500cc's | 750cc's | 3000cc's |

To determine the displacement, subtract .045 inches from the bore measurement and multiply the difference by itself. Multiply the product by .7854 and multiply the continued product by the stroke and the number of cylinders.

In designating class, the frame classification is first, followed by a dash, then the engine classification, an-

** *Altered engines unlimited in design, but made by a motorcycle manufacturer.*

other dash, and finally the displacement. A typical number plate would look like: APS-AG-350, to be found on the side of a bike with a modified frame and partial streamlining. Its modified gas burning engine would have a displacement of 350cc's.

Let's look at the records:

| Class | C.C. | Cu. In. | M.P.H. | Make | Code | Date Set |
|---|---|---|---|---|---|---|
| C-C | 50 | 3 | 64.470 | Suzuki | 1 | 8-29-70 |
| C-AG | 50 | 3 | 58.788 | Suzuki | 2 | 8-24-70 |
| A-C | 50 | 3 | 38.577 | Honda | 5 | 8-23-69 |
| A-AG | 50 | 3 | 72.588 | Suzuki | 6 | 8-22-69 |
| A-A | 50 | 3 | 78.947 | Suzuki | 7 | 8-18-69 |
| APS-AG | 50 | 3 | 75.364 | Suzuki | 14 | 8-29-70 |
| APS-A | 50 | 3 | 82.264 | Suzuki | 15 | 8-24-70 |
| S-AB | 50 | 3 | 121.700 | NSU | 20 | 8-9-56 |
| C-C | 100 | 6.1 | 82.822 | Kawasaki | 1 | 8-24-70 |
| C-AG | 100 | 6.1 | 80.026 | Honda | 2 | 8-23-69 |
| C-A | 100 | 6.1 | 73.194 | Hodaka | 3 | 8-26-70 |
| A-C | 100 | 6.1 | 83.561 | Bridgestone | 5 | 10-22-68 |
| A-AG | 100 | 6.1 | 90.078 | Suzuki | 6 | 8-25-70 |
| A-A | 100 | 6.1 | 91.639 | Suzuki | 7 | 8-26-70 |
| PS-C | 100 | 6.1 | 76.681 | Yamaha | 9 | 8-25-66 |
| PS-A | 100 | 6.1 | 73.251 | Kawasaki | 11 | 8-25-67 |
| APS-C | 100 | 6.1 | 81.103 | Yamaha | 13 | 8-23-66 |
| APS-AG | 100 | 6.1 | 95.728 | Suzuki | 14 | 8-29-70 |
| APS-A | 100 | 6.1 | 87.489 | Honda | 15 | 8-20-69 |
| S-C | 100 | 6.1 | 101.225 | Yamaha | 17 | 8-19-69 |
| S-AG | 100 | 6.1 | 113.249 | Bridgestone | 18 | 10-25-68 |
| S-A | 100 | 6.1 | 138.000 | NSU | 19 | 8-3-56 |
| C-C | 125 | 7.6 | 84.077 | Bultaco | 1 | 8-26-66 |
| C-AG | 125 | 7.6 | 78.432 | Yamaha | 2 | 8-26-70 |
| C-A | 125 | 7.6 | 82.270 | Yamaha | 3 | 8-24-70 |
| A-C | 125 | 7.6 | 75.573 | Suzuki | 5 | 8-26-70 |
| A-AG | 125 | 7.6 | 91.214 | Yamaha | 6 | 8-20-69 |
| A-A | 125 | 7.6 | 102.094 | Honda DOHC | 7 | 8-25-66 |
| PS-A | 125 | 7.6 | 90.318 | Bultaco | 11 | 8-28-64 |
| APS-A | 125 | 7.6 | 107.577 | Honda DOHC | 15 | 8-24-66 |
| S-A | 125 | 7.6 | 15.000 | NSU | 19 | 8-2-56 |
| C-C | 175 | 10.4 | 87.087 | Kawasaki | 1 | 8-24-67 |
| C-AG | 175 | 10.4 | 76.633 | Kawasaki | 2 | 8-24-70 |

| Class | C.C. | Cu. In. | M.P.H. | Make | Code | Date Set |
|---|---|---|---|---|---|---|
| C-A | 175 | 10.4 | 89.361 | Kawasaki | 3 | 8-25-67 |
| A-C | 175 | 10.4 | 90.187 | Kawasaki | 5 | 8-25-67 |
| A-AG | 175 | 10.4 | 92.512 | Kawasaki | 6 | 10-23-68 |
| A-A | 175 | 10.4 | 100.905 | Honda DOHC | 7 | 8-23-66 |
| PS-C | 175 | 10.4 | 101.617 | Ducati | 9 | 8-28-65 |
| PS-A | 175 | 10.4 | 90.623 | Kawasaki | 11 | 8-25-67 |
| APS-C | 175 | 10.4 | 101.251 | Bridgestone | 13 | 8-19-69 |
| APS-AG | 175 | 10.4 | 99.515 | Honda DOHC | 14 | 8-29-70 |
| APS-A | 175 | 10.4 | 111.941 | Honda DOHC | 15 | 8-22-66 |
| S-A | 175 | 10.4 | 150.000 | NSU | 19 | 8-2-56 |
| C-C | 200 | 12.2 | 104.833 | Yamaha | 1 | 8-24-70 |
| C-AG | 200 | 12.2 | 88.203 | Honda | 2 | 8-25-70 |
| C-A | 200 | 12.2 | 104.341 | Yamaha | 3 | 8-26-70 |
| A-C | 200 | 12.2 | 96.434 | Suzuki | 5 | 8-29-70 |
| A-AG | 200 | 12.2 | 104.271 | Honda DOHC | 6 | 8-25-70 |
| A-A | 200 | 12.2 | 104.733 | Honda DOHC | 7 | 8-26-70 |
| PS-C | 200 | 12.2 | 112.115 | Yamaha | 9 | 8-26-70 |
| PS-A | 200 | 12.2 | 95.824 | Bridgestone | 11 | 10-24-68 |
| APS-C | 200 | 12.2 | 103.866 | Bultaco | 13 | 8-18-65 |
| APS-AG | 200 | 12.2 | 110.411 | Honda DOHC | 14 | 8-24-70 |
| S-C | 200 | 12.2 | 139.820 | Triumph | 17 | 9-6-59 |
| C-C | 250 | 15.2 | 125.854 | Suzuki | 1 | 8-22-69 |
| C-A | 250 | 15.2 | 125.567 | Yamaha | 3 | 8-24-70 |
| A-C | 250 | 15.2 | 128.096 | Yamaha | 5 | 8-26-70 |
| A-A | 250 | 15.2 | 125.306 | Yamaha | 7 | 8-25-70 |
| PS-C | 250 | 15.2 | 130.117 | Suzuki | 9 | 8-20-69 |
| PS-AG | 250 | 15.2 | 11.714 | Yamaha | 10 | 8-28-70 |
| PS-A | 250 | 15.2 | 132.771 | Suzuki | 11 | 8-23-70 |
| APS-C | 250 | 15.2 | 133.060 | Yamaha | 13 | 8-29-70 |
| APS-AG | 250 | 15.2 | 113.365 | Suzuki | 14 | 8-28-70 |
| APS-A | 250 | 15.2 | 122.296 | Kawasaki | 15 | 8-26-67 |
| S-C | 250 | 15.2 | 176.824 | Harley | 17 | 10-22-65 |
| S-A | 250 | 15.2 | 150.000 | NSU | 19 | 8-2-56 |
| C-C | 350 | 21.3 | 125.698 | Bridgestone | 1 | 10-24-69 |
| C-A | 350 | 21.3 | 120.802 | Triumph | 3 | 8-27-60 |
| A-C | 350 | 21.3 | 100.685 | Kawasaki | 5 | 8-29-70 |
| A-AG | 350 | 21.3 | 105.121 | Bridgestone | 6 | 8-25-70 |
| A-A | 350 | 21.3 | 120.317 | Honda | 7 | 8-22-69 |
| PS-C | 350 | 21.3 | 150.266 | Yamaha | 9 | 8-19-69 |
| PS-A | 350 | 21.3 | 145.732 | Yamaha | 11 | 8-24-70 |
| APS-C | 350 | 21.3 | 146.221 | Bridgestone | 13 | 8-29-70 |
| APS-AG | 350 | 21.3 | 115.329 | Honda | 14 | 8-24-70 |
| APS-A | 350 | 21.3 | 126.304 | Honda DOHC | 15 | 8-28-65 |
| S-C | 350 | 21.3 | 197.813 | Yamaha | 17 | 9-18-70 |
| S-A | 350 | 21.3 | 193.756 | Yamaha | 19 | 9-18-70 |
| S-AB | 350 | 21.3 | 189.500 | NSU | 20 | 8-8-56 |

| Class | C.C. | Cu. In. | M.P.H. | Make | Code | Date Set |
|-------|------|---------|--------|------|------|----------|
| C-C | 500 | 30.5 | 142.650 | Suzuki | 1 | 8-21-69 |
| C-AG | 500 | 30.5 | 124.763 | Kawasaki | 2 | 8-29-70 |
| C-A | 500 | 30.5 | 123.370 | Kawasaki | 3 | 8-21-69 |
| A-C | 500 | 30.5 | 134.320 | Suzuki | 5 | 8-29-70 |
| A-AG | 500 | 30.5 | 116.654 | Honda | 6 | 8-21-69 |
| A-A | 500 | 30.5 | 132.875 | Kawasaki | 7 | 8-23-69 |
| PS-C | 500 | 30.5 | 147.153 | Suzuki | 9 | 8-20-69 |
| PS-AG | 500 | 30.5 | 101.608 | Honda | 10 | 8-23-69 |
| PS-A | 500 | 30.5 | 148.884 | Suzuki | 11 | 8-23-69 |
| APS-C | 500 | 30.5 | 137.362 | Kawasaki | 13 | 8-26-70 |
| APS-AG | 500 | 30.5 | 126.379 | Norton OHC | 14 | 8-22-69 |
| APS-A | 500 | 30.5 | 146.889 | Kawasaki | 15 | 8-29-70 |
| S-A | 500 | 30.5 | 212.278 | Triumph | 19 | 8-28-58 |
| C-A | 600 | 36.6 | 92.551 | Kawasaki | 3 | 8-29-70 |
| S-C | 600 | 36.6 | 179.304 | Norton | 17 | 8-25-61 |
| C-C | 650 | 40 | 147.420 | Triumph | 1 | 8-28-58 |
| C-AG | 650 | 40 | 114.904 | BSA | 2 | 8-19-69 |
| C-A | 650 | 40 | 146.266 | Triumph | 3 | 8-23-66 |
| A-C | 650 | 40 | 129.966 | Triumph | 5 | 10-23-68 |
| A-AG | 650 | 40 | 120.223 | BSA | 6 | 8-28-70 |
| A-A | 650 | 40 | 159.542 | Triumph | 7 | 8-25-61 |
| PS-C | 650 | 40 | 140.541 | Triumph | 9 | 8-27-66 |
| APS-C | 650 | 40 | 130.938 | Triumph | 13 | 8-26-70 |
| APS-A | 650 | 40 | 161.793 | Triumph | 15 | 8-29-65 |
| S-C | 650 | 40 | 205.785 | Triumph | 17 | 8-22-62 |
| S-A | 650 | 40 | 230.269 | Triumph | 19 | 8-24-62 |
| C-C | 700 | 42.7 | 114.432 | Enfield | 1 | 8-26-70 |
| PS-C | 700 | 42.7 | 115.631 | Enfield | 9 | 8-29-70 |
| PS-A | 700 | 42.7 | 141.879 | Enfield | 11 | 10-23-68 |
| APS-AG | 700 | 42.7 | 132.296 | Rickman Tri. | 14 | 8-29-70 |
| APS-AB | 700 | 42.7 | 128.640 | Triumph | 16 | 8-28-64 |
| S-AG | 700 | 42.7 | 251.924 | 2-Eng. Yama | 18 | 9-17-70 |
| S-A | 700 | 42.7 | 192.436 | 2-Eng. Yama | 19 | 8-29-70 |
| C-C | 750 | 45.7 | 142.382 | Triumph 3 | 1 | 8-24-70 |
| C-AG | 750 | 45.7 | 136.249 | Triumph 3 | 2 | 8-22-69 |
| C-A | 750 | 45.7 | 139.871 | Triumph 3 | 3 | 8-20-69 |
| C-AB | 750 | 45.7 | 133.379 | Triumph 3 | 4 | 8-19-69 |
| A-C | 750 | 45.7 | 141.569 | Triumph 3 | 5 | 8-22-69 |
| A-AG | 750 | 45.7 | 144.481 | Triumph 3 | 6 | 8-23-69 |
| A-A | 750 | 45.7 | 158.126 | Enfield 3 | 7 | 8-22-69 |
| A-AB | 750 | 45.7 | 146.733 | BSA 3 | 8 | 8-29-70 |
| PS-C | 750 | 45.7 | 147.723 | Triumph 3 | 9 | 8-23-69 |
| PS-AG | 750 | 45.7 | 145.650 | Triumph 3 | 10 | 8-21-69 |

| Class | C.C. | Cu. In. | M.P.H. | Make | Code | Date Set |
|-------|------|---------|--------|------|------|----------|
| PS-A | 750 | 45.7 | 142.406 | Triumph 3 | 11 | 8-21-69 |
| PS-AB | 750 | 45.7 | 138.451 | Triumph 3 | 12 | 8-18-69 |
| APS-C | 750 | 45.7 | 148.323 | Triumph 3 | 13 | 8-21-69 |
| APS-AG | 750 | 45.7 | 145.567 | Triumph 3 | 14 | 8-22-69 |
| APS-A | 750 | 45.7 | 169.331 | Triumph 3 | 15 | 8-23-69 |
| APS-AB | 750 | 45.7 | 151.407 | Triumph 3 | 16 | 8-23-69 |
| S-AG | 750 | 45.7 | 208.729 | Norton | 18 | 8-29-70 |
| S-A | 750 | 45.7 | 221.742 | Triumph 3 | 19 | 8-22-69 |
| | | | | | | |
| C-C | 883 | 55 | 142.828 | Harley | 1 | 8-22-63 |
| C-AG | 883 | 55 | 130.250 | Honda 4 | 2 | 8-25-70 |
| A-C | 883 | 55 | 135.682 | Harley | 5 | 8-22-69 |
| A-AG | 883 | 55 | 123.309 | Honda 4 | 6 | 8-28-70 |
| A-A | 883 | 55 | 143.939 | Triumph 3 | 7 | 8-29-70 |
| PS-A | 883 | 55 | 149.443 | Harley | 11 | 8-23-63 |
| APS-C | 883 | 55 | 132.093 | Harley | 13 | 8-23-69 |
| APS-AG | 883 | 55 | 130.843 | Harley | 14 | 8-22-69 |
| S-A | 883 | 55 | 178.971 | Indian OHV | 19 | 8-20-62 |
| | | | | | | |
| C-C | 1000 | 61 | 147.580 | Vincent | 1 | 9-6-53 |
| C-AG | 1000 | 61 | 137.702 | Honda 4 | 2 | 8-28-70 |
| C-A | 1000 | 61 | 140.642 | Harley | 3 | 8-26-66 |
| A-AG | 1000 | 61 | 137.215 | Honda 4 | 6 | 8-29-70 |
| A-A | 1000 | 61 | 160.739 | Vincent | 7 | 9-10-53 |
| A-AB | 1000 | 61 | 164.308 | Vincent | 8 | 8-22-63 |
| PS-A | 1000 | 61 | 138.170 | Harley | 11 | 8-25-66 |
| APS-AG | 1000 | 61 | 149.285 | BSA 3 | 14 | 8-25-70 |
| APS-A | 1000 | 61 | 148.956 | BSA 3 | 15 | 8-29-70 |
| S-A | 1000 | 61 | 183.586 | Indian OHV | 19 | 8-25-67 |
| | | | | | | |
| C-C | 1200 | 74 | 134.278 | Harley | 1 | 8-28-70 |
| C-AG | 1200 | 74 | 150.470 | Harley | 2 | 8-23-69 |
| C-A | 1200 | 74 | 141.742 | Harley | 3 | 8-26-67 |
| A-AG | 1200 | 74 | 141.242 | Harley | 6 | 8-22-69 |
| A-A | 1200 | 74 | 146.230 | Harley | 7 | 8-1-57 |
| PS-C | 1200 | 74 | 126.756 | Harley | 9 | 8-21-63 |
| PS-AG | 1200 | 74 | 160.222 | Harley | 10 | 8-20-69 |
| PS-A | 1200 | 74 | 141.041 | Harley | 11 | 8-25-67 |
| APS-AG | 1200 | 74 | 139.781 | Harley | 14 | 8-23-69 |
| | | | | | | |
| C-AG | 3000 | 183 | 155.833 | Harley | 2 | 10-25-68 |
| C-A | 3000 | 183 | 186.731 | Harley | 3 | 8-29-70 |
| A-AG | 3000 | 183 | 155.578 | Harley | 6 | 8-29-70 |
| A-A | 3000 | 183 | 194.724 | Enfield | 7 | 8-26-70 |
| A-AB | 3000 | 183 | 172.455 | Harley | 8 | 8-29-70 |
| PS-AG | 3000 | 183 | 162.164 | Harley | 10 | 8-18-69 |
| PS-A | 3000 | 183 | 202.379 | Harley | 11 | 8-25-70 |

| Class | C.C. | Cu. In. | M.P.H. | Make | Code | Date Set |
|-------|------|---------|--------|------|------|----------|
| APS-AG | 3000 | 183 | 169.604 | Harley | 14 | 8-24-70 |
| APS-A | 3000 | 183 | 190.596 | Harley | 15 | 8-23-69 |
| S-A | 3000 | 183 | 245.667 | 2-Eng. Tri | 19 | 8-25-66 |

While there are now 169 established records, there is a possible 320, which means that all you have to do in one of the other 151 classes to set a world's record is to show up with something that qualifies. Try it. Perhaps the next book you buy will have your name in the record section.

## OTHER

Another facet of the racing scene records the abilities of the riders themselves. Under a National Point System professional riders are given a number of prescribed number of points for every race they complete. The winner receives the greatest number of points. Second, third, fourth, fifth and other place riders receive lesser points. At the end of each season the rider with the most points becomes the year's Grand National Champion and the following season races with the numeral 1.

### AMERICAN MOTORCYCLE ASSOCIATION GRAND NATIONAL CHAMPIONS

| 1946 | Chet Dykgraaf | Norton |
|------|---------------|--------|
| 1947 | Jimmy Chann | Harley-Davidson |
| 1948 | Jimmy Chann | Harley-Davidson |
| 1949 | Jimmy Chann | Harley-Davidson |
| 1950 | Larry Headrick | Harley-Davidson |
| 1951 | Bobby Hill | Indian |
| 1952 | Bobby Hill | Indian |
| 1953 | Bill Tuman | Indian |
| 1954 | Joe Leonard | Harley-Davidson |
| 1955 | Brad Andres | Harley-Davidson |

| 1956 | Joe Leonard | Harley-Davidson |
| 1957 | Joe Leonard | Harley-Davidson |
| 1958 | Carroll Resweber | Harley-Davidson |
| 1959 | Carroll Resweber | Harley-Davidson |
| 1960 | Carroll Resweber | Harley-Davidson |
| 1961 | Carroll Resweber | Harley-Davidson |
| 1962 | Bart Markel | Harley-Davidson |
| 1963 | Dick Mann | BSA-Matchless |
| 1964 | Roger Reiman | Harley-Davidson |
| 1965 | Bart Markel | Harley-Davidson |
| 1966 | Bart Markel | Harley-Davidson |
| 1967 | Gary Nixon | Triumph |
| 1968 | Gary Nixon | Triumph |
| 1969 | Mert Lawwill | Harley-Davidson |
| 1970 | Gene Romero | Triumph |

In addition, there is a National Enduro Championship and a National Hillclimb Championship. The Grand National Champion is determined after the riders have participated in the Dirt Track and Speedway events, Short Track events, TT (Tourist Trophy) events and Road Races. The riders are separated according to their ability and performance into three groups: Expert, Amateur and Novice. The events are further divided according to the displacement of the machines competing. From 0-250cc's is lightweight, and from 251-750cc's is heavyweight. Experts and Amateurs may ride in either division, Novices are restricted to lightweight.

The AMA says, "An enduro is a contest where speed is not the determining factor and wherein a time schedule has to be maintained. . . ." It's held over little-used roads, trails, footpaths, and a variety of other kinds of country where a motorcycle can be taken under its own power or (again AMA), "the muscular energy of the rider."

A further amendment says that it can't include more than 24 hours of continuous riding and must have at least two rest stops of one-half hour each. A 24-hour event is known as a Two-Day run, and must cover at least 300 miles without covering the same ground more than four times.

There are two rider classes, A and B. A rider remains in the B class until he has amassed 200 points, at which time he is made an A rider.

There are six categories within the two classes:

I Class A:

| | |
|---|---|
| Lightweight | 0-200cc's |
| Mediumweight | 201cc's-350cc's |
| Light-Heavyweight | 351cc's-600cc's |
| Heavyweight | 601cc's + |
| Sidecar | any size |
| Buddy Seat | any size |

II Class B:

| | |
|---|---|
| Bantamweight | 0-100cc's |
| Lightweight | 101cc's-200cc's |
| Mediumweight | 201cc's-250cc's |
| Light-Heavyweight | 251cc's-500cc's |
| Heavyweight | 501cc's + |
| Sidecar | any size |
| Buddy Seat | any size |

### AMERICAN MOTORCYCLE ASSOCIATION NATIONAL CHAMPION ENDURO RIDERS

| | | |
|---|---|---|
| 1962 | Bill Baird | Triumph |
| 1963 | Bill Baird | Triumph |
| 1964 | Bill Baird | Triumph |
| 1965 | Bill Baird | Triumph |
| 1966 | Bill Baird | Triumph |
| 1967 | Bill Baird | Triumph |
| 1968 | Bill Baird | Triumph |
| 1969 | John Penton | Husqvarna |
| 1970 | Jack McLane | Honda |

A Hillclimb can be a series of runs against a distance on a steep hill, or a race against time to the top of a hill. The hill must be at least 20 feet and not more than 25 feet wide.

A rider becomes National Champion after receiving the most points at the end of a season of Hillclimb events.

Again there are A and B riders, determined in the same manner as in Enduro events.

## AMERICAN MOTORCYCLE ASSOCIATION CLASS A HILLCLIMB NATIONAL CHAMPIONS

| | | | |
|---|---|---|---|
| 1953 | Class A | Howard Mitzel | Indian |
| | Class B | Duane Nealen | Indian |
| 1954 | Class A | R. Nealen | Indian |
| | Class B | Duane Nealen | Indian |
| 1955 | Class A | R. Nealen | Indian |
| | Class B | Louis Corriere | Harley-Davidson |
| 1956 | Class A | Howard Mitzel | Indian |
| | Class B | Phil Rockwell | Indian |
| 1957 | Class A | Duane Nealen | Indian |
| | Class B | Charles Jacobs | Triumph |
| 1958 | Class A | Earl Buck | Ariel |
| | Class B | Gordon Mitzel | Indian |
| 1959 | Class A | Joe Hemmis | Triumph |
| | Class B | Harold Warner | Harley-Davidson |
| 1960 | Class A | Charles Jacobs | Harley-Davidson |
| | Class B | Vic Salvador | Indian |
| 1961 | Class A | Charles Jacobs | Harley-Davidson |
| | Class B | Paul Mayer | Indian |
| 1962 | Class A | Joe Hemmis | Triumph |
| | Class B | Phillip Petrick | Harley-Davidson |
| 1963 | Class A | Glen Kyle | Vincent |
| | Class B | Phil Petrick | Harley-Davidson |
| 1964 | Class A | Joe Hemmis | Triumph |
| | Class B | Tom Reiser | Harley-Davidson |
| 1965 | Class A | Glen Kyle | Vincent |
| | Class B | Beese Wendt | Indian |
| 1966 | Class A | Glen Kyle | Vincent |
| | Class B | Beese Wendt | Indian |
| 1967 | Class A | Joe Hemmis | Triumph |
| | Class B | Jack Taylor | Harley-Davidson |
| 1968 | Class A | Earl Bowlby | BSA |
| | Class B | Jack Taylor | Harley-Davidson |

| 1969 | Class A | Beese Wendt | Vincent |
| | Class B | Doyle Disbennett | BSA |
| 1970 | Class A | Carl Wickstrand | Triumph |
| | Class B | Jim Thompson | BSA |

Chapter 12

## *1971 PROFESSIONAL RACERS:*

### The Top Ten Riders Make Up
### 1971's List of Racers to Watch

ONE OF THE MOST gut-sports in the world is motorcycle
racing. Once you've seen 20 riders hurtling around a
dirt track, sliding through the turns and careening into
walls at more than 100 miles an hour; or once you've
witnessed a band of 50 riders braking wildly at more
than 150 miles an hour as a turn rushed toward them,
you know for certain those are men.

There are many riders of this caliber in races across
the country; of that number each year, ten distinguish
themselves above all others. Perhaps the ten fall a little
less, go a little faster or brake for corners a little later
than the others. They are the "men to beat" the next
time around. They are the "men to watch" by the
people who regularly go to the races. They are the best.

The men to beat and the men to watch in 1971—the
ten top riders of the year—are:

1. Gene Romero
2. Jim Rice
3. David Aldana
4. Dick Mann
5. Don Castro
6. Mert Lawill
7. Mark Brelsford
8. Chuck Palmgren
9. Tom Rockwood
10. Gary Nixon

Rider standings are determined by a point system developed by the AMA which covers all of their National Races. Points are awarded on the basis of the importance of the race run, which is decided by the amount of prize money paid in the Expert division. That's a bit different from last year, and the scale is as shown on page 167.

The 1970 champion circuit included four road races, nine half-mile races, two short track races, five TT races, and five one-mile track races held over a period of nine months in every part of the country. Altogether they paid over a quarter of a million dollars in prize money, without including contingencies and bonuses given by the bike manufacturers.

Last year started on February 6th in the Houston Astrodome with an indoor TT race. Jim Rice took first, on his BSA, followed by Paul Bostrom on a Triumph and Skip Van Leeuwen, also riding a Triumph.

That was followed the next night by an indoor short track race which found Mert Lawwill riding his Harley across the line first with Dick Mann and his Ossa and James Odom with Bultaco coming across second and third, respectively.

March brought the famous Daytona 200 Miler and a new record of 102.691 set by Dick Mann with a 750cc Honda four. Gene Romero piloted his Triumph to second with his Triumph teammate, Don Castro, breathing down his neck for third.

At that point Mann was first with 122 points, Romero was next with 91, and Castro was third with 82. But the season had just begun.

The next championship race was on April 6th in Seattle where the experts got together for a race. A Suzuki ridden by Ron Grant came in first, with second going to Yvon Du Hamel of Canada who rides a Yamaha. Third went to ex-number one, Gary Nixon.

# NATIONAL POINT SYSTEM
## Scale "A"

| Positions | $15,000 or more | $12,000 to $14,999 | $10,000 to $11,999 | $9,000 to $9,999 | $8,000 to $8,999 | $7,000 to $7,999 | up to $6,999 |
|---|---|---|---|---|---|---|---|
| 1 | 101 | 86 | 71 | 62 | 53 | 30 | 26 |
| 2 | 91 | 76 | 61 | 52 | 43 | 16 | 19 |
| 3 | 82 | 67 | 52 | 42 | 34 | 14 | 13 |
| 4 | 74 | 59 | 44 | 35 | 26 | 12 | 9 |
| 5 | 67 | 52 | 37 | 28 | 19 | 10 | 8 |
| 6 | 61 | 46 | 31 | 22 | 12 | 8 | 7 |
| 7 | 56 | 41 | 26 | 17 | 8 | 6 | 6 |
| 8 | 52 | 37 | 22 | 13 | 5 | 5 | 5 |
| 9 | 49 | 34 | 19 | 10 | 4 | 4 | 4 |
| 10 | 46 | 31 | 16 | 7 | 3 | 3 | 3 |
| 11 | 43 | 28 | 13 | 4 | 2 | 2 | 2 |
| 12 | 40 | 25 | 10 | 1 | 1 | 1 | 1 |
| 13 | 37 | 22 | 7 | | | | |
| 14 | 34 | 19 | 4 | | | | |
| 15 | 31 | 16 | 1 | | | | |
| 16 | 28 | 13 | | | | | |
| 17 | 25 | 10 | | | | | |
| 18 | 22 | 7 | | | | | |
| 19 | 19 | 4 | | | | | |
| 20 | 16 | 1 | | | | | |
| 21 | 13 | | | | | | |
| 22 | 10 | | | | | | |
| 23 | 7 | | | | | | |
| 24 | 4 | | | | | | |
| 25 | 1 | | | | | | |

Palmetto, Georgia, hosted the next big event, a half-mile dirt track race on April 19th. Jim Rice and his BSA came in first in this one too, followed by another

BSA ridden by Dick Mann and a Norton under Jack Warren. It was the season for half milers and Cumberland, Maryland, was the scene of the next one on May 3rd. Mert Lawwill came in first this time piloting a Harley with Dave Aldana on BSA and Larry Palmgren with Triumph taking second and third, respectively.

The standings to that point found Dick Mann still in the lead with 165 points, Yvon Du Hamel second with 117, Mert Lawwill a close third with 110 challenged by the 106 points of Jim Rice.

Talladega was the sight of the next National points competition with a road race that found Dave Aldana putting on an inspired show to take first with his BSA traveling at an average speed of 104.589mph. Jody Nicholas on a Suzuki came in second and Jim Rice found third with his BSA. Aldana's phenomenal win had put him in second place behind Mann.

The Reading, Pennsylvania, half-mile event ended May with Rice winning to take second place Nationally with his BSA while Larry Palmgren pushed his Triumph to third and Dick Mann got enough points from his third place to keep his national lead with 245 points.

Next was the June half-mile at Louisville Downs that saw a Canadian named Dave Sehl ride his Harley Davidson to first. Calvin Rayborn, his teammate, took second while Larry Palmgren got into the picture with his Triumph for third.

June 14th brought Louden (ex-Laconia, a rather famous race on the circuit) which Gary Nixon and Triumph put away. Second was Dave Smith with a Kawasaki while Don Emde brought his Yamaha in for third. Then came the TT at Santa Fe Park in Illinois. Eddie Mulder, who seems to have a corner on the TT market took this one too, with his Triumph, while fellow Triumph rider, Skip Van Leeuwenn took second. Chuck

Palmgren took his Yamaha for a good ride and third place.

Now Mann was first in points, Rice second, and Aldana third. All of them riding BSA's.

Next on the circuit was the Charity Newsies National Championship, held at Columbus, Ohio. Dave Sehl, the Canadian who won the Louisville race, took the honors here, too. Ronnie Rall, a local boy in big-time racing came in second on a BSA and Larry Palmgren's Triumph carried him across for a third. Down the list at sixth was Jim Rice, who received enough points to take over the overall standings from Dick Mann.

San Jose on the West Coast was the site of the next big one, and July 5th found Rice and his BSA putting another first away and advancing his points lead. Second at San Jose went to Jim Odom on Triumph while Yamaha and Chuck Palmgren took third.

Then it was North to Castle Rock, Washington, and a championship TT. Dick Mann came roaring back into the picture to take it on his BSA, Don Castro on Triumph was second and young Mark Brelsford, racing for Harley-Davidson, found the right track for third. Mann's victory put him back in first by a 25 point margin over second place Jim Rice. Aldana moved over to let Gene Romero grab third in the national points race.

On the 18th of July, famous Ascot Park hosted a national points TT at its home in Gardena, California. Harley-Davidson's Mert Lawwill had a spectacular show to bring home first, Gene Romero drove a good race and took second place with his efforts, and a local racer aboard a BSA, Dallas Baker, was third.

A mile race at the Santa Rosa, California, track eight days later went to Jim Rice (BSA), with Jim Odom taking second on a Triumph and Chuck Palmgren bringing his Yamaha around the bend for third.

Racers and fans got an unusual three-week layoff when the half-mile at Tulare was canceled because a heavy rain had loosened the track surface so much that AMA officials decided it was too dangerous for competition. So the next race was held in the east at Terre Haute, Indiana, on August 16th. It was a half-mile that made BSA people very happy when David Aldana came in first and Jim Rice was second. Yamaha was third again, this time piloted by Keith Mashburn.

The 21st of August Bart Markel brought his Harley in first at the Santa Fe Park short track. In doing so the veteran racer tied the all-time Championship wins record with a career total of 27. Jim Rice rode his BSA in for a second and Yamaha and Neil Keen paired for third.

Jim Rice was again the leader with 397 points, Dick Mann held second only eight points below with 389, Gene Romero had a remote 332 points, and Dave Aldana was 102 points behind with 295.

But places shifted rapidly after the next race, the Peoria TT. Jim Rice rode his BSA across the line first for his sixth win of the season, Dave Aldana was aboard a slightly slower BSA and took second, and Triumph's Gene Romero picked up third.

Then came the August 30th race, a miler at Sedalia, Missouri. Gene Romero had his first win of the season and another Triumph bearing Don Castro was second. Leader Jim Rice was third on his BSA, which gave him enough points to stay first nationally, but Gene Romero was right behind him for second. Dick Mann, third in point standing, dropped his bike during the race and dropped out of contention with a broken leg.

Another miler was run on September 6th in Nazareth, Pennsylvania; this time Chuck Palmgren ran his

Yamaha for a first, followed by Gary Nixon and his Triumph teammate, Don Castro, in second and third places respectively.

The next night Indianapolis, Indiana was the sight of the third miler. Dave Aldana set a new track record to win first with his BSA. Triumph riders Tom Rockwood and Larry Palmgren followed up with second and third. Now Aldana was fourth.

The end of the season was closing fast when the deciding race was held in Sacramento, California.

The bikes were impressive. Harley-Davidson was running their 750cc twin, the XR 750 Eliminator with four separate oil coolers since they had had trouble with overheating earlier in the season. BSA was there with twins and three's. Some liked the twins, others— notably Jim Rice, a top contender—rode the three. Dave Aldana rode a Rocket, too. Triumph had the same selection for their riders. Gene Romero preferred the lighter twin, Gary Nixon rode a Trident.

Yamaha's 650 was much in evidence, generally put into a Trackmaster dirt racing frame. There were some Nortons there too, in Trackmaster frames.

Every top rider in the nation was there, hoping to win, and knowing that they had to beat Rice and Romero, either of whom would win the 1970 championship with a first in Sacramento.

Gene Romero, a young Californian who had won only one championship race all season yet was second in national points with 521, rode a Triumph twin. Jim Rice, young and also a Californian, had won six championship races and was ahead in points (534). He rode a BSA three. Dick Mann had removed his cast early, and rode his BSA to the second fastest qualifying time. Mert Lawwill and Cal Rayborn, both on Harleys, were ready to go. Rice's partner, Dave Aldana, had his BSA sharpened up; but so did Triumph's stiff competition Castro, Nixon and Tom Rockwood. And there for Yamaha was Chuck Palmgren.

Romero ran in the first qualifying heat and set the fastest time of the day with a 40.60 second lap.

Mann recorded the second fastest time of the day in the second heat—41.10 seconds. Mert Lawwill won the third heat.

In the fourth heat, Jimmy Odom and Gary Nixon on Triumphs came in first and second and Jim Rice qualified for the main by coming in third. As Rice was shutting down and going into the turn where I was standing taking pictures, he missed a gear and lost it. At about 100 miles per hour. Rice flew face-first into the guard rail, somehow managing to come away with only a broken nose and minor lacerations. His bike flew sideways over the hay bales and guard rail, swept through the air and crashed into me.

Jim, with the help of admirable stamina and a pit crew that pieced his machine together as best it could, raced in the main event.

With the help of nine broken ribs, a broken shoulder and a lung contusion, I spent the next two weeks in a hospital bed with a respirator.

And so the all-important race started. Dave Aldana, another BSA team man, dropped his bike in the first lap and couldn't get it started while Gene Romero leaped ahead at the start to take the lead. Dick Mann stuck it out a while but finally quit when his still broken leg became too much to bear. Mert Lawwill's Harley went down under the strain and he finished tenth. Jody Nicholas, who qualified with the third fastest time on his Norton broke an oil line and was forced out.

Gary Nixon performed like the champion he has twice been in years past, sliding his heavy Trident through the turns with a ferocious racing style that made him a crowd pleaser until his crankcase caught on the track and dumped him in the 48th lap. That's hard luck in a 50-lap race.

The Sacramento mile race ended with Gene Romero never having been out of first place. Tom Rockwood, also on a Triumph came in second and Cal Rayborn on a Harley-Davidson took third.

The standings from there, with the 101 points Romero got for first place, were:

| | | |
|---|---|---|
| 1. | Gene Romero | 622 |
| 2. | Jim Rice | 565 |
| 3. | Dave Aldana | 443 |
| 4. | Dick Mann | 412 |
| 5. | Don Castro | 379 |
| 6. | Mert Lawwill | 317 |
| 7. | Chuck Palmgren | 303 |
| 8. | Tom Rockford | 294 |
| 9. | Mark Brelsford | 272 |
| 10. | Gary Nixon | 268 |

The Sacramento race put Gene out of reach of the other racers but left quite a bit of room for jockeying for position among the runner-up nine.

The next race was a half mile at Gardena, California, which Gene won, too. Mark Brelsford brought his Harley-Davidson through for a second place while Lloyd Hutchins rode a Triumph in for third.

The season officially ended on October 4th, two days short of nine months from the day it started, at the Oklahoma City fairground's half-mile track. Mark Brelsford rode his Harley to a win, Romero came in second, and his teammate Larry Palmgren was third.

It was a hard-fought season, with no racer giving an inch. Every point won was due to the skill of the rider and the dedication of the pit crews (and a small margin of luck). Each man asked more of himself in this season than many men get from themselves in a lifetime.

Let's take a look at them.

## Gene Romero

Gene started racing at 18, the youngest permissible age according to AMA regulations. He's been in the forefront of racing since that first season, placing in the top ten consistently. Last year he was number three, behind Mert Lawwill and Dick Mann, both of whom are older and have been racing longer.

Unlike several men in the top ten, Gene doesn't divide his time among other pursuits. Some people list as their professions a second field: sales representative, machinist, motorcycle sales, and most often, mechanic. But Gene concentrates on racing.

He has developed a smooth style. It doesn't depend on ferocious riding or chance taking. Instead he squirts from the line to get the best position he can, and then rides smoothly and consistently, pushing the people ahead of him and leaving the people behind him way behind.

A style like this takes years of practice and experience to work. With too little experience you push too hard and try to take advantage of openings that are too small and you lose. Or you don't push hard enough.

Last year it didn't work quite right and Gene was third. This year he pushed just a bit harder and he won the championship with two national victories.

Gene comes from California, as do eight of the top ten riders this year. He's 5'8" tall and weighs 168 pounds—heavier than any of the other riders in the top ten.

## Jim Rice

Jim is another Californian who started racing early

and has just kept going up. He is only 22 and waited until last year to turn pro. After proving himself the first season, he was invited to become part of the BSA factory team.

During the off-season, he spends his time working on bikes. He has an ability that many of the best racers have, a talented aptitude for mechanics.

On the track, Rice is a picture of intense concentration. On the line he looks mad until the flag drops, and then he cranks the throttle and no one can see what his face looks like from the back of his helmet.

His riding style is explosive. If he starts at the front of a pack he stays there no matter what the cost, riding fast—sometimes faster than necessary—until he wins or falls. If he starts at the back of the pack he fights his way toward the front.

Jim's style is the opposite of Romero's, because he seems to be driven by a "win or bust" urge that makes him take chances. As a result, he won six national races this season, and still scored second because his nonwins were complete losses.

Jim, too, is a big man, at 5'11" and 160 pounds, winning a small man's sport.

### Dave Aldana

Three racers, three Californians. Dave is the third, calling Santa Ana home when professional racing gives him enough time to have a home.

Dave turned professional at 18 too, after four years of racing that began when, at 14, he competed on a 50cc Suzuki. He was given a boost toward the field by his father who had raced as a sportsman, and his uncle who was and is a tuner. Racing excited him, but amateur division was too tame, and he was about to quit when a call from BSA brought him back.

It is unusual for a racer to place as high as third in

national points competition during his first year with the experts, and the rider who does indicates he has a wealth of natural talent.

Dave seems to be good at all sorts of racing—he's won road races, TT's, and dirt track races—with a violent style all his own. He hits the course with everything he's got and demands the same of his bike. He can take the lead, and even if it were only a three-lap lead he wouldn't call it comfortable until he had won. He drives like a madman, yet a look at his record will tell you he wins a lot, too. Experience will bring smoothness, which is all he needs to claim the number one spot.

Dave is typical of winning racers; he is small (5'5") and light (135 lbs.). And he's got guts.

### Dick Mann

The oldest man in the top ten has been among those ten for some time. He's 36-year-old Dick Mann, who seems indestructible in his 18th year of competition.

This year saw him tying the all-time record for number of national points races won—next year he'll beat it. It's impossible to count Dick out in any type of race, since he's won just about every type. Road racing has provided most of his victories but flat track, oval dirt races of all lengths, and TT's have all given up a first to him.

This year at Sacramento, Dick showed up alone, acting as his own pit crew and doctor, since he had to cut himself out of a cast in order to race. A wreck a little earlier in the season fractured his leg badly, and would have kept anyone else down.

It is that kind of endurance and dedication that has won him a National Championship and placed him in the top ten for ten straight years.

## Don Castro

Don, another young Californian, has been plagued by bad luck but seems to be making out in spite of it. Last year in his first year as a professional, he was out for the first half of the season with a broken ankle. Halfway through the season he began racing again, with such a vengeance that he won six nationals. His style varies, and it will have to be enough to characterize it as "effective." I'm in good company in making that evaluation. At the beginning of his second professional year, Triumph came to the same conclusion and signed him on as a team member.

Don, only 20, comes from Hollister, California, where the draft board has his name on an induction notice that may put a temporary kink in his racing career.

## Mert Lawwill

Mert is a 29-year-old San Franciscan who's been racing since he was 19. Last year he capped his career by winning the number one spot for himself and Harley-Davidson. Prior to that win he had been ranked in the top ten for five straight years.

In addition to racing, Mert is a mechanic, a trade that comes in handy when he races.

Mert Lawwill is small too, standing 5'6" and weighing only 138 pounds.

## Mark Brelsford

Mark began his racing career by hurtling around local tracks in his home town of San Bruno on a 50cc Honda. Today, five years later, Mark is 20 and has been racing professionally for two years.

Last year he was put into eighth place nationally, and made the Harley-Davidson racing team as a starter. This year saw him rise to seventh, and with a natural talent for throwing big bikes rapidly around race courses, he could jump to first next season. Certainly without injury he will never be out of the top ten.

Besides racing, Mark lists himself as a student. It's difficult to believe that anyone who studies cycle racing as devoutly as Mark has time for anything else. During the little time he has off, Mark races at the indoor short track at the San Francisco Cow Palace.

Mark is the lightest of all the riders, weighing in at 125 pounds, which seems to be just the right weight for winning on a Harley-Davidson.

## Chuck Palmgren

Chuck is one of three Palmgren brothers in cycle racing. Larry races for enjoyment, and although he doesn't enter all the races he wins a startling percentage of those he does enter. Last year he entered ten races and finished in the money in all of them to be ninth ranked in national points.

Chuck's younger brother, Dennis, is now racing and there may be a day not far off when the name Palmgren will appear in the top ten three times.

This year Chuck is responsible for putting it there. He is one of two top riders not from California. Chuck lives in Freehold, New Jersey and has taken advantage of the tutelage of ex-Champion Gary Nixon to incorporate Nixon's best tricks into his own style. He rides a Yamaha and is best on dirt tracks where he has brought his Yamaha to victory in National Championship Competition many times with inspired riding.

## Gary Nixon

The name Gary Nixon has a magic of its own around U.S. tracks where his cycle riding prowess is known and respected by everyone. He took the national championship twice in a row, but on his third attempt his luck ran out. He crashed into a retaining fence at Santa Rosa in midseason and fractured his right leg. So high was his point score by then that without competing in any more events he still made ninth in the national rating.

This year he took it easy, concentrating only on the road events until he regains full use of the leg. Even so he wound up taking tenth to bring up the rear of the top ten.

He rides Triumph in the big bike classes and a Yamaha in the smaller classes, training a number of aspiring young racers at the same time.

There they are: the top ten. The next time you watch a race, watch for these men. They will be where the action is.

Chapter 13

## CYCLE CAMPING:

### A Few How To's, What To's, and What-Not-To's That Will Help Make Cycle Camping the Fun It Should Be

TWO OF MY FAVORITE SPORTS are cycling and camping and I'm typical of many riders in that. The fact that I've chosen a bike that rides best off the highway only proves the point. But my first camping experience was launched with more enthusiasm than knowledge. Even though I carried enough equipment to supply five campers, I was cold at night, hot during the day, underfed at mealtime and dissatisfied with what could have been a lot of fun.

Since then I've learned how to get along with less equipment and I've learned how to learn from other campers. I've swapped ideas over many campfires and little by little I've learned ways to make a good camp.

If you are a veteran of camping campaigns, skim through this chapter to pick up anything new or helpful. But if 1971 will be your first attempt at camping, read what I have to say. The things I've learned could help to avoid the pitfalls I made.

## Plan Ahead

Decide where you are going in advance. Then write letters for information. Write to the Chamber of Commerce in towns around the area and gather data on State and National Forests. They make good camping areas. If you are going to be on Bureau of Land Management land or in a National Park write to them. They can offer advice. And if you are leaving the state write ahead for the vehicle laws in each state you plan to visit. Ask the Department of Motor Vehicles for regulations on helmets, lights and mufflers.

Explain what you want to do and where you plan to go. Ask for maps, travel guides, camping regulations and fire restrictions. An idea that has helped me a great deal is to ask advice from the person to whom you are writing. As a resident he knows some of the things many people don't. The extra edge may make a difference in camping comfort. Always include a stamped, self-addressed envelope with your inquiry.

If your destination is several days off, you have two choices on the road: you can camp out or stay in motels. The answer depends on the kind of travel you like and the money you have—but camping is best. If you plan to camp buy a campground directory at your local bookstore or get in touch with a campground chain such as KOA (Kampgrounds of America) to find out where you can stay enroute. If you are riding on a busy weekend like the Fourth of July or Labor Day make reservations well in advance. If you plan to stay in motels make reservations for the return trip as well. It is easy to do if you stay with one chain since they usually have a reservation service that will take care of it quickly.

In any event decide on a time for stopping—then

stop. Don't try to milk a few more miles from a late sunset. You may end up in a dark stretch of highway with no place to stay but alongside the road.

## Tents

The image of an old woodsman does not include a tent, but then the image also avoids rain, snow and heavy dew. Perhaps the woodsman can get away without a tent but you, your gear and your bike can't.

My tent is a two-man nylon back-packer with a sewn-in floor and a nylon fly at the top. I own a two-man tent even though I usually camp alone because I like to keep my gear close and dry. It makes a great difference when I wake up to face a cold morning with dry clothes. A two-man tent also saves food from marauding pests.

The sewn-in floor is insurance against a late night rain that has taken a path which invariably ends somewhere in your sleeping bag. Even when it doesn't rain a fully enclosed shelter is warmer than one without a floor.

Canvas is the most durable, but is also heavy and bulky. It is really not worth considering for cycle camping. Plastic is weatherproof, light and compact, but not very durable. Nylon has all of the advantages of plastic with almost the durability of canvas. Be sure the kind you buy is water repellent—there is a difference between water repellent and water resistant. And ask for rip-stop material. Rip-stop nylon is quilted like tinfoil. The sheet is divided into hundreds of tiny squares and when punctured will not tear through more than one square.

The fly is a piece of nylon that stretches over the tent to protect it from water, falling debris such as pinecones and acorns and anything that might tear the material. The fly is inexpensive and lasts one season before it is discarded—much cheaper than discarding tents annually.

Erect your tent once before you leave. Break it down without removing any of the guy ropes after they have been adjusted. It makes it easier to set the tent up a second time. Bring your own stakes and don't forget to include a hatchet with a blunt side for driving the stakes.

If you want to make an economy tent make one from a sheet of plastic or nylon. Again, set it up once at home before you go just to be sure everything works. If you need help a Boy Scout manual is a lifesaver.

Since your cycle makes up half of the camping adventure, don't forget a cover. Almost all bike shops carry compact, lightweight covers. Don't forget it: a cover can keep your ignition system dry in a driving rain.

## Sleeping Gear

Your sleeping gear is the most important part of your equipment and if you are extravagant with nothing else, go all the way in this. I have a down-filled mummy bag I swear by. It's nylon covered and will keep me comfortable in zero weather. It comes in a stuff-sack that reduces its size to a small cylinder. At night the sleeper unrolls and I fill the bag with my clothes. It makes a good pillow.

Down-filled bags are the warmest. Second are polyester-filled versions and the others are generally too heavy or bulky for cycling. If you anticipate weather colder than that for which your bag is designed, you can add ten degrees of protection by inserting a flannel inner liner. You can make one at home for very little.

If you are not using a tent bring a waterproof ground

cover. Sleep on it and put your equipment on it at night to keep shoes, socks and personal items dry.

The choice between air mattress and a sleeping pad is a matter of personal preference. I use a pad and find that in addition to being softer, it keeps me warmer. There are two types of pads: rippled and smooth. The ripple surface is supposed to be cooler in summer, but I've only used the smooth type and do recommend it.

Air mattresses do not insulate as well as pads, but are as comfortable. Save money and trouble by purchasing the very best in the beginning. Order a reinforced rubber mattress rather than a light plastic type.

## Stoves, Heaters and Lights

In many areas the warm weather that makes camping good also increases the fire danger. At critical levels authorities forbid open campfires in all but established campgrounds. In most cases you will be prepared for all eventualities if you carry a stove.

Like most campers I prefer to cook over an open fire. It adds to the atmosphere and the flavor of the food, but often open fires are prohibited. I make it a practice to bring a stove no matter where I go.

There are several types of fuels available. Bottled gas (Humphrey, Bernz-O-Matic and others), pressurized fuel (the familiar Coleman type), drawn gas (Primus and Optimus) and canned fuel (as Sterno and Fire Ribbon).

Fire Ribbon comes in a toothpaste tube. Squeeze a little in the bottom of a can and light. By the time it burns out the contents of the can are heated. Open the can before you light the material.

Canned fuels are becoming more popular. They are often used now with a collapsible stand which keeps the pot at a proper height above the flame. Complete kits with fuel, stand and instructions are sold at many outdoors shops. The best kits include pot, pan, lid and cup as well.

I don't take a heater with me because they are bulky, costly and consume space, but some riders I know won't travel without them. If you need one take a look at the catalytic heaters. Several good manufacturers make them and you can get them in round, flat and square shapes.

If your trip is short you can get by with a flashlight for lighting (bring spare batteries), but if you plan an extended jaunt a flashlight is impractical for anything except emergencies. Several manufacturers make pressurized lanterns which are good for car camping, but do not work well with a bike. The mantles are so fragile they break under vibration. I was stopped until I met some Sierra Club hikers who showed me the device I use to this day. It is a collapsible box, tin on top and bottom and glass on the other sides. When a candle is put inside it gives enough light for all camp chores.

## Utensils

Don't overdo it. Remember when you get an urge to add something extra that utensils take up a surprising amount of room and anything you don't need is just extra weight. There are excellent cooking kits with everything included. With a little effort you can find one with equipment you consider "minimal." Buy it, carry it, use it. My kit has a small pot, a frying pan and a cover I use for a plate. I've added one fork, a good hunting knife and a spoon.

I also carry a Sierra Club cup, available nearly everywhere: it hooks on your belt and is ready at all times. In addition I have a small canteen and a collapsible five-gallon plastic tank with a spigot. I can fill it with water when I reach camp. Be sure to include a first-aid kit. You can buy ready-assembled kits but let your doctor pick it out. There are too many cheap ones on the market. Add a snake bite kit if your first aid box doesn't have it. If mosquitoes bother you, add insect repellent. In addition, "first aid" for your bike should include spare gas, a change of plugs, a set of good tools, wire (plus electrical wire), a chain breaker and link and tube patching kit.

## Food

Don't carry excess food, but don't stint. Forget perishables and concentrate on high energy foods. I use the new dehydrated and freeze-dried foods. After deciding on the length of my trip, I compute the number of meals involved and plan the menu. I try to include most items before I leave, buying only those few fresh foods I'll want—milk, lettuce, etc.

I bring pouches of vitamin C reinforced fruit juices for drinking in camp and add powdered milk for breakfast. When the ingredients are purchased I pack them in my kit. In many cases I save room by removing the food from boxes and storing it in plastic bags. When I do this I include the rear pannel from the original box with its cooking instructions. For breakfasts I often carry eggs (in special plastic containers available from hiking shops) and I like dehydrated foods such as those found in packing and climbing shops.

For maximum energy and nutrition I buy foods from a natural food store (although I'm not a food addict). Granola is great (a natural grain cereal with honey flavoring). Often I add uncooked nuts, roasted soy beans, sunflower seeds and dried fruits. They take up less space than most foods and supply all the nutrition I need. Sometimes I mix them all together: the result is a good-tasting, prepared meal that can't spoil. It is sold commercially in many shops as GROP, but you can make your own for less money. For clean-up add a small amount of bio-degradable soap—not a detergent—and when you clean the dishes at night spill it onto the ground, not into the stream.

## Packing

If you own a bike with a single seat you are in luck but if you own a rig with a dual seat you have to improvise. If you plan to do much camping switch the large seat for a single. The greatest invention for campers is the pack rack which can be attached to the back of any single seat machine. Buy the chrome type which cannot rust. The best types have a lip in back and be sure the rack includes small metal projections for tie-downs.

Hard saddle bags, called panniers, are fine for the road but won't work in rough country. Even leather types have been ripped apart by limbs, rocks and brush. Soft packs are better and you can try either canvas saddle bags or a back pack. Mine is a nylon back pack with an adjustable aluminum frame, padded shoulder straps and a waist band. I prefer the pack because once you reach your destination it can be used for carrying equipment in day trips by foot.

My pack frame has a mount at the bottom for a sleeping bag, so I put mine there. The tent and pad (with the pad wrapped in its ground cover) are rolled tightly and independently, then added. I use rope tie downs, but shock cord will work as well.

I pack the smaller items in the back of the rack, against the lip. Then the sleeping pad and tent. The gas can goes on its side and then the rest of the gear. I adjust the pack so that the bottom rests on the seat while I am riding—that is, looser than when I am hiking. I tie everything down and I'm ready to leave. Tools and repair parts should be packed near the top so you can reach them quickly if you need them. A map also helps and it's most easily usable if you tape it to your fuel tank.

## Clothes

My own rule is: always add insulated clothing. A parka is first. It keeps me warm in cold weather yet isn't too hot when the sun comes out. Bring two pairs of jeans or heavy pants, three pairs of socks, two T-shirts and a warm wool jacket.

Wear boots. Not a pair of sneakers, not oxfords, but boots—boots with cleated soles. Add heavy socks and your feet will be comfortable under all circumstances. If the shoes are not waterproofed, buy a commercial waterproofing preparation and use it. The effort will pay off during the first rain or at the first stream.

If the cost of outfitting seems high, haunt surplus stores. You can find almost everything I've mentioned there. All that's left is the fun and that's up to you. But if you have any questions don't look for me. I've gone camping.